S0-EKL-918

Investing for Beginners

Daniel O'Shea

Financial Times Business Information

© *Daniel O'Shea 1982, 1983, 1984, 1985, 1986*

Material in **Investing for Beginners** is copyright and may not be reproduced in whole or in part for any purpose nor used in any form of advertising or promotion without the written permission of the publishers.

Published by
Financial Times Business Information Limited.
102 Clerkenwell Road
London EC1M 5SA
Registered Number 980896

Typeset by Graphac Typesetting, Wimbledon, London SW19 1RH
Printed by The University Press, Oxford.
ISBN 0 902101 854

First published 1982
Reprinted with amendments 1983
Second edition 1984
Reprinted with amendments 1985
Third edition 1986.

Contents

Preface

This is a book which focuses on the stockmarket, though it also covers unit trusts, life assurance and other indirect investment media. It emerges with an established history: the joint parent is the influential weekly investment magazine, *Investors Chronicle*. It saw the light of day in the following way.

Early in 1981 Michael Brett, then editor of the *Investors Chronicle*, asked me to write a series of articles on investment, aimed at taking the beginner right through the subject from scratch. His idea was that in the years since the *Investors Chronicle's* original *Beginners Please* book had been written, there had been an entirely new generation of investors and a new approach was needed.

He consulted me since he knew I had helped to write and edit the last edition of *Beginners Please* when working with him on the *Investors Chronicle*. Since 1973 I have been looking at investment from a different corner as research director with M & G, the unit trust and investment group. This combination of experience, he thought, was the right one for the job. I agreed to take it on.

The articles were published weekly over a period of roughly a year under the general title of 'Beginners Guide'. Their immediate popularity meant that a book based on the full series of articles became an obvious sequel.

So this is it. In fact, a considerable amount of work has been necessary to adapt to the book form. I have added a completely new section on Capital Gains Tax. And I have compiled a glossary of investment terms which not only supplements the text but acts as a source of cross reference. The latest edition has been revised to reflect the investment events since then, notably the change in Stock Exchange procedures (the 'Big Bang') and the Personal Equity Plans.

Nonetheless, the framework of the book is basically the 'Beginners Guide' series. I owe much to the guidance and help provided by Michael Brett, who himself wrote the original sections on property shares and on traded options.

Daniel O'Shea

1

How safe are stocks and shares?

Not as safe as a savings account, potentially far more profitable but also far more risky. What are the risks, and how can they be reduced?

Whenever you make a choice about where to put your money, you are explicitly or implicitly asking yourself the question: how can I get the maximum return with the minimum risk? Certainly anybody who acts as an investment adviser has the task of breaking down the queries about money into these components.

Of course, everybody always does want the maximum return. But many of us also want security of capital and/or income. At each end of the spectrum, these two aspirations are irreconcilable.

The greatest security of capital is, for most people, to keep the money in some form of savings account – at worst you get in money terms what you put in, even if inflation has eroded its real value meanwhile. In capital terms, the 'Granny Bond' is now an alternative. But savings accounts do not give very high returns. Even the Granny Bond, though guaranteed to keep up with the retail price index, does not offer anything much in excess of this.

At the other end of the scale, anyone who launches himself out into business on his own, based on his life savings, and perhaps with borrowed money as well, is obviously going for the maximum return and is equally clearly devoid of any security.

Between these two lie a host of options. The most universally adopted compromise is, as a first step, to own your own house, on borrowed money. The return has been historically high, in tangible and intangible forms. The risks – apart from the fact that you may leave yourself without a roof over your head if you cash in on your investment – are of course those associated with borrowing and those associated with the value of the house. The two are interconnected and nobody who has been a householder over recent years needs reminding of them.

However, once you have invested in your own house, and put what you think you will need into an easily cashable form for regular or emergency use, you have to ask yourself more specific questions about risk and reward. And the answer for most people is some form of purchase of shares or gilt-edged stock – in other words, quoted stockmarket investments.

Risk in individual shares

Before we go into the mechanics of this, ask yourself what your aims are in the context of risk and reward. And to start at the top end of the spectrum, we can point to some share performances over recent years, particularly in certain North Sea oil exploration companies and small electronics groups, where you could have made your fortune by concentrating your money in one share. Equally, you could have lost most or all of it if you had purchased the wrong one.

Descending the scale somewhat, you could have confined your investment to a single company which nonetheless was evidently large and successful. Again, time might have brought you considerable gains in certain shares, but considerable losses in others.

Spread reduces risk
Alternatively, you could have opted for a package of shares (a 'portfolio' in the jargon of the trade) in a more or less representative sample of some or all of the aspects of the UK economy. You could have purchased the shares in your own right, or chosen an investment or unit trust which effectively manages a spread of shares on your behalf. The wider your spread of investment, the nearer you would approach the general performance of the UK stockmarket. Your risks would have been reduced; so would your rewards.

Even the rewards of a very widely spread portfolio have been reasonable in recent years. As I write (late 1986) the UK stockmarket, as measured by the FT-Actuaries All-Share Index, is well over twice what it was five years ago. Many portfolios, managed by individuals, by their stockbrokers, or by unit or investment trust managers, have done better than this, but even taking this stockmarket index you would have beaten most forms of savings.

However, our knowledge of the last five years does not entitle us automatically to assume the same sort of return in future. The risk in share investment not only lies in the selection of shares, which can be reduced by a wider spread, but also in the timing of purchases. Shares in general fluctuate, sometimes widely, over the short and medium term. If they are bought when the market is low and sold when it is high, very high returns have been demonstrated. But in the nature of things nobody can ever be quite certain when the peaks and troughs are going to occur.

This risk of timing is something which marks out shares from savings deposits, and it is usually the most fundamental reason for the average person's reluctance to put his money into the stockmarket. It can't be waved away, but it can be reduced.

Reducing the risks of timing
One way – the obvious one – is to be prepared to commit your funds for a much longer period than with a deposit. Share investment is best regarded as longer term, even if subsequently it proves to be good in a shorter period. Another way, which is also a longer-term option, is to carry out an automatic and regular series of purchases instead of plunging in at one go. You can do this by taking out a regular commitment with one of the unit trust groups which administer such series. By this means, you will iron out the effects of the peaks and the troughs on the value of your shares.

Of course, by the same token you will lessen the profit you might have earned by correct, or lucky, timing and choice of investment had you relied on your own judgment. So here we must add another element which will reduce your risk and yet, one hopes, will give you a better return. That element is knowledge. You can never learn enough about companies, shares, the stockmarket and its behaviour. None of us ever has, or ever can. The more background you can acquire, the better should be your investment results. This is not a risky statement to make!

2
How gilt-edged stocks work

Gilt-edged stocks have a guaranteed interest rate and often a guaranteed repayment at a fixed date. But they still involve some risk, because their market prices fluctuate.

There are two main types of investment quoted on the Stock Exchange: shares, or 'equities' as they are often called, and Government securities, usually known as 'gilt-edged' stock. There are other types but they are not important in this context.

Gilt-edged stocks derive their name from the paper on which notes of the most impeccable kind were issued in the early days of stock exchanges. The name implies that the Government guarantees to pay a fixed sum in interest each year, and in the case of most stocks guarantees to repay the stock on a certain date at 'par' – that is, £100 repayment for every £100 stock originally issued. (There are now also certain gilt-edged stocks which are 'index-linked', with a different kind of guarantee, which I will refer to later.)

Clearly, gilt-edged stocks are completely different from shares, where no guarantees of this kind are given. In this sense, gilt-edged are more akin to building society or bank deposits. The security of repayment is, technically, even greater than with banks or building societies since it is always possible (though highly unlikely) for one of the latter to 'go bust'. The security of gilt-edged is that of, say, a National Savings Certificate. Are there any risks in gilt-edged investments?

The inflation risk of gilts
There are two types of risk. The first is in common with all forms of fixed interest deposits and savings media. If you buy a gilt-edged stock and keep it until the official repayment date, your return is fixed and it will not necessarily compensate you for inflation over the intervening period.

In fact over most of the period since the end of World War II, gilt-edged were disastrous investments. In recent years, as inflation has been recognised as the menace that it is, the fixed returns on gilt-edged stocks offered by the Government on new issues of stock have been raised. They have, in these recent years, tended to stand at levels which, if inflation had continued at the rate assumed by most people, would have given you a return just about in pace with that inflation, depending on your tax rate and the sort of gilt-edged stock you bought. But if inflation should rise beyond this, you would lose on the deal.

The second risk with gilt-edged is that, unlike a deposit, the stocks are actually quoted in the market, and fluctuate in value according to the trends and conditions of the economy and the balance between buyers and sellers. In the short term, therefore, they carry the same sort of risk as shares, though not in the same degree.

There are many reasons for the fluctuations in gilt-edged market prices. The most important one is the trend in interest rates generally. Over any longish period, if inflation is seen to be rising, interest rates will also rise. The reverse is also true. But how does this affect gilt-edged prices?

Let us take an example from one particular stock – Treasury 9 per cent 1994. This stock was issued some years ago, at a price which was designed to give the right rate of interest at the time. Let us assume that the issue price was £100. The guarantee is that stockholders will get £9 each year in interest payments, and will be repaid at £100 in 1994. But interest rates (that is, the rates paid on all forms of deposits and the returns on savings) subsequently rose. Over the years since the issue, interest rates have several times been at higher levels. At one point, when interest rates were around 12 per cent in 1982, it stood at about £74 per original £100 issued. You still got your £9 per year, but the annual return on the market value was about 12 per cent. This, given all the circumstances, was deemed to be the 'right' current yield, allowing for the fact that you would also have obtained an extra £26 in capital when the stock is repaid.

With the exception of irredeemable stocks, which have no repayment date, all the other gilt-edged stocks, of which there are a large number, with various repayment dates and 'coupons' (i.e. fixed annual payments) are influenced in the same way. Some of them, which are due for early repayment, may stand nearer to the 'par' value, and would then have yielded less than this figure of 12 per cent, depending on how large the coupon is for the period up to repayment, and therefore on how much of the return between now and then will be free of income tax. For the capital gain element as the stock price rises towards the date when it is repaid is not taxed.

When gilts become attractive
Naturally, when interest rates are falling, gilt-edged market prices will tend to rise.

For example, if interest rates dropped from 12 per cent to 9 per cent over twelve months, in theory our Treasury 9 per cent 1994 should follow the trend, and be yielding around 9 per cent. The market price would have to rise to £100 to do this, and you would thus have achieved a capital profit of £26 over the year, as well as your £9 coupon. (In fact, interest rates *did* drop over 1982/83, and by early 1983 this stock was quoted at £91, to yield about 10 per cent, in line with the fall in interest rates).

In this sense, since interest rates are affected by inflation expectations, an investment in gilt-edged is a sort of bet on inflation coming down further over the long-term. As I mentioned earlier, the course of gilt-edged from 1946 until the last few years has been a disaster for investors. Some investors feel we may now be in a phase where there is some chance of a permanent reduction in inflation, and therefore of a real profit to the gilt-edged holders. You must make your own minds up about this.

INDEX-LINKED GILT-EDGED
Since the Budget of 1982, the private investor has been able to buy index-linked gilt-edged stocks, which were formerly only available to pension

funds. There are, so far, eleven of these stocks with redemption dates spanning the period from 1988 to 2020. Their coupons are either of 2 or 2½ per cent.

These stocks have two guarantees. The first is that the coupon payments will be raised each year (actually each six months) by reference to the Retail Price Index. The second is that the stocks will be repaid at the redemption dates appointed, at their issue price plus the inflation in between, again as measured by the Retail Price Index. There is no guarantee in money terms. If retail prices _go down_ so will the redemption price.

The difference between these stocks and the National Savings 'Granny Bonds' is twofold. First there is the promise of index-linked income, albeit at a very low starting level. Second, there is no capital indexing until the date of redemptions and no 'fall-back' of the sum deposited. The stocks are quoted in the stockmarket, just like conventional gilt-edged. They are therefore subject to ups and downs in supply and demand. If inflation falls, the value of the stock will fall, because the market will take a lower view of the likely redemption price. If at some future date, investors start to assume a continuous decline in inflation, or even an actual fall in prices, they might not want to buy the stocks at anything like the earlier market prices, so these could look very sickly indeed.

Conventional gilts and index-linked gilts, therefore, are both differing bets on the future course of inflation over the period of investment. If inflation stays at stable levels (whatever those levels may be at any one time) you are likely to get the sort of return obtainable on a fixed deposit. In a conventional gilt, you will get this through the coupon plus whatever the fixed price on redemption may contribute as a premium. In indexed gilts you will get the return through the indexed repayment plus the element of steady coupon increase. At any one time the market prices of the stock will reflect investors' views on the prospects and will allow for the expected future inflation.

If inflation falls more than is expected, you will make some real profit on conventional gilts, but a monetary loss on index-linked. If inflation rises more than expected, you will lose on conventional gilts.

The best ultimate outcome for conventional gilts would be a world super-slump; for index-linked gilts, it would be hyperinflation.

3

Equities give you a piece of the action

Ordinary shares – equities – carry greater risks than gilt-edged stocks, partly because the shareholder's fortunes are linked so closely with those of the company he invests in, but the possible returns are greater.

The middle course is where shares, or equities, come in. They will of course suffer from any profound extreme in economic and financial troubles. But in any likely 'scenario', they offer a chance to benefit from inflationary conditions, or from declining inflation. History shows they can do well in both conditions, through the falling general price levels of the 1930s, the early post-war period of moderate inflation, and the most recent period of high inflation.

However, shares do suffer shocks from rapid changes in conditions. Like the companies which they represent, they take time to adjust. There are also natural fluctuations in economic affairs, which reflect on share prices in a more volatile way than upon gilts. This is why it is difficult to take a really representative period in measuring share performance. Going back too far into the past may be unrepresentative of recent trends; yet too short a period is also unsatisfactory for other reasons.

One particular year in recent history, 1974, adds an additional complication to the records. The long-term index chart on page 8 shows how extreme was the movement both down and then up, over 1974 and 1975. I firmly believe that this extraordinary phenomenon will not occur again in our lifetime. This was when the full impact of the first oil crisis hit Britain, when we had not yet produced oil, and when the Government did just about everything wrong, all at the same time.

Another difficulty about demonstrating a representative performance in shares is that an index (even a very good index such as the Financial Times Actuaries All Share Index) does not tell you what an actual collection of shares (a 'portfolio') would have done, where the holder has selected shares and avoided some of the worst market effects.

So, to cover some of these difficulties, I have taken four 'funds' over four periods. The first fund is the FT/A All Share Index, with income reinvested after standard or basic rate tax. The second is the FT Government Securities Index, again with net income reinvested. The third is a real fund, the M & G Second General Trust, a unit trust which is not an exceptional performer, but a steady 'middle of the road' fund, typical of many. The fourth is simply the cost of living as measured by the Retail Price Index.

The four periods, all finishing at June 30, 1986, are of 5, 10, 15 and 20 years. The five year period, starting in 1981, is part of the bull market of recent years. The ten year period, starting in 1976, began at a lowish level after the fall of 1974. The fifteen year period began about half-way through the bull market which ended in 1972-73.

Four funds' performance over four periods to 1 July 1986; capital and income reinvested after basic rate tax.

'Fund'	5 years %	10 years %	15 years %	20 years %
FT/A All Share Index	+200	+660	+728	+1,309
FT Government Securities	+89	+168	+193	+233
M & G Second General Trust Fund	+200	+763	+1,151	+1,937
Cost of Living	+30	+147	+380	+531

The figures are as shown in the table. You can get an idea of where the periods start from the chart of the two indices, produced by stockbrokers de Zoete & Bevan. One is of their own equity index, and the other of their gilt-edged index. This chart also gives you a very long-term picture covering one great period of deflation and one of inflation.

de ZOETE EQUITY PRICE INDEX AND de ZOETE GILT PRICE INDEX

Any specific period of comparison, where markets are concerned, can give a distorting view. Clearly, the 10 year period, starting after a market fall, is one of these. Nonetheless, I think that the long term chart and the performance records demonstrate how equities are ultimately likely to be a better 'two way bet' than conventional gilts, and probably better than index-linked gilts also.

What is a share?

A share is, almost literally, a 'piece of the action'. All public companies have a defined amount of issued equity capital, which is divided up into shares of a particular nominal 'par' value. This may be £1, 50p, 25p or other denominations. The most popular unit nowadays is 25p. This is the par value which the *Financial Times*, in its back pages of share prices, assumes to be the case if nothing else is specified.

Thus a company may have an issued capital of £1m divided into 25p shares, making 4m shares in all. But what matters far more than the par value of a share is its market value – what you can actually buy and sell it for. The market value of shares will not necessarily correspond to their par value; in fact it will in most cases almost certainly be higher, reflecting the growth of the company and the return given by its dividends to shareholders.

In an unquoted company, this value has to be established by a process which can be rather haphazard. In their early stages, small companies may have only a very small number of shareholders and the problem of how to transfer ownership at the 'right' price is difficult.

As companies grow, and their ownership widens, the solution to this problem is to seek a quotation for the shares; either unofficially (in the case of, say, a relatively small local company) or, more imperatively when growth has been considerable, by an official Stock Exchange listing.

However large or small, however many shares are issued, the key word applicable to a share is still 'ownership'. Although the founder of a company, and his family, may still hold a large number of its shares, even the most modest 'outside' shareholder, as soon as he has purchased his shares on the market, has the same property as the founding family, in proportion to his own holding. The fortunes of that company, for good or ill, will then be shared by him, the dividends distributed will come to him, exactly in proportion.

Other kinds of shares

There are *some* types of share which do not carry exactly similar rights and privileges to others. In certain companies, where the original owners have sought to maintain their control of the company despite the issue of shares to outsiders, there are classes of shares without a vote in any company general meeting. These are sometimes referred to as 'A' shares, and are specified as such in the *Financial Times* quotation pages. I would not encourage anyone to buy such shares. The rights of ownership ought to include participation in voting. In crucial cases, such as in takeover bids, the lack of a vote can be a disadvantage.

There are other types of share which are not significant in the context of this discussion. One of these is the deferred share, where dividends are restricted. Another is the preference share, which is really a fixed interest stock and not an 'equity'. Yet another is the convertible stock, a hybrid form of investment which I shall look at in a later chapter. How you go about buying and selling of shares I leave to my next chapter.

4

How to buy and sell stocks and shares

The costs of buying and selling in the stockmarket – and some hints on finding a stockbroker.

The Stock Exchange is a market and is like any other place where goods are traded, so far as the final bargain is concerned. But it is also subject to a series of rules, dating back to its origins and modified over the years, which are designed to observe fairness to all the parties concerned. These rules have been altered as from October 1986, but for the private investor the basics still remain similar. The biggest difference is that commission charges are no longer fixed by the Stock Exchange.

There are two basic functions within this market. The first is performed by by what used to be called the 'jobbers' and which are now referred to as 'market makers'. They hold trading positions in the stocks and shares, in the same way as any stall holder in a street market. In other words they buy (or sell) shares with their own money in the hope they can sell (or buy) them afterwards at a profit. There are a number of firms who tend to specialise in particular groups of stocks.

The market makers set the prices of the stocks or shares they deal in according to supply and demand.

Variations in this will of course change the quotation as a whole, and there are very few days when actively traded stocks do not fluctuate in this way. There will be no exact correspondence between the price you see in the paper and the price at which you buy and sell therefore, and how much variation you wish to tolerate is part of your decision to deal.

Finding a stockbroker
As a private individual you are unlikely to buy a share directly from a market maker. For this, you would be better to go to a stockbroker, or to somebody who deals with one.

Stockbroking firms are many times more numerous than market makers, and they come in all sizes from huge diversified groups with many specialities, to the two- or three-partner firm. Throughout the UK there are local firms, who tend to be smaller in size than their more numerous London counterparts.

There are indeed five regional Stock Exchanges, which used to be distinct from London, but which are now linked in one body. Many regional stockbroking firms have either a direct or indirect presence in London, too.

Nowadays, stockbrokers are allowed to advertise, but not many of them do so. The traditional method of finding a stockbroker by 'knowing someone' is still probably the commonest. In this, your bank manager may well be a useful guide, because he may directly or indirectly use a number of firms in the course of bank business, and he may also provide the introduction on which all personal relationships (the essence of stockbroking) depend.

However, you may also get a list of stockbrokers who are willing to take on small investors from the Stock Exchange itself, either the London one or any of the Regional exchanges in Glasgow, Liverpool, Birmingham, York or Belfast.

What will you pay for the services of your stockbroker? The costs of investing on the Stock Exchange come cheapest if you buy gilt-edged stock. Commission used to be 0.8 per cent on bargains up to £2,500. Under the new rules this may vary, but it is unlikely to be very different. There will be a minimum charge, which used to be £7, and this again may vary, most probably being higher.

Shares are a different case. To begin with, all buyers of shares (not sellers) have to pay Transfer Stamp Duty. This is to the Government not to the broker, but is a significant element of the cost, at 0.5 per cent on the total value of the bargain.

Stockbrokers' commission as such used to be at a standard rate of 1.65 per cent on bargains up to £7,000 with further reductions on amounts hardly relevant to the small investor. On 'small bargains', there was a minimum commission of £10. It is not difficult to appreciate that *any* deal involves an irreducible minimum of costs. In some cases, even £10 is unlikely to be enough to cover the full amount.

Thus, to buy in too small a lump sum can be relatively costly. You can work out that at any bargain less than £600 the £10 charge begins to represent more than the old standard rate. Under the new Stock Exchange rules, you may choose to go to a stockbroker who charges very low commission or no commission at all. But if you want service and advice, you will always have some charge to pay. No visible commission does not mean that your deal is without cost. And for small deals there will almost always be a minimum fee of some kind.

Gilts through the Post Office
Small buyers of gilts should always consider the Post Office, who keep a list of approved stocks and charge very low fees for small bargains which they will undertake for you.

There are other relatively minor charges involved in any bargain: there is Contract Stamp (a maximum of 60p), Stock Exchange Levy (60p, only on bargains of over £5,000) and VAT on the commission.

Thus, without involving the extra weighting on a small bargain, your overall Stock Exchange costs over the life of a share investment (i.e. covering purchase and eventual sale) will be a significant sum if you are only dealing over short periods, allowing for the fact that both the stockbroker and the market maker will be adding their own margins. And therefore a 'profit' on an investment is unlikely to be a profit until it starts to clear 10 per cent on the back page of the *Financial Times!*

Buying your shares
The method of payment has not altered fundamentally over the years, despite the streamlining of the machinery. Once you have established yourself with a

stockbroker, you may quite simply telephone him with an order to buy whatever shares you wish.

You will have to confirm with him what the price of the shares is, on the Stock Exchange, at that point. It may not be the same as in yesterday's newspaper. If you agree with the price, you may go ahead and give your order. You may want a lower price, in which case you may leave instructions with the broker to buy at such a price if the shares fall. Your broker will usually be able to tell you whether this is likely or not, and whether you decide to proceed is then up to you.

If you do proceed, your broker will subsequently confirm with you that your order has been carried out. The next communication you get will be your contract note, which is the most important item of your investment file. It records the deal, with the price per share, the commission or any other comparable fee, the Stamp Duty, and the total amount involved. Different stockbrokers have different styles, but the format is basically the same. The contract note is your reference for Capital Gains Tax, as well as a vital part of your own records.

The Stock Exchange 'Account'
The contract note is also your bill: but it does not have to be paid immediately. The Stock Exchange operates a system of accounts for share transactions, which is currently a two-week period but under the new rules will eventually become shorter. Your stockbroker will inform you as to the method of payment.

The reason for the account is that it enables the large and diverse dealings of all the members of this very special 'club' to be carried out in the most practical manner. No market maker or broker could cope with the same turnover on a cash payment system. Gilt-edged dealings have to be for cash but then these are comparatively uncomplicated. So regardless of how many transactions take place, payment does not complicate the issue within the account, and indeed many of the movements involved are netted out by market makers and brokers into single payments covering multiple transactions.

What applies for the members also applies for their clients. All your transactions in shares within the account, though recorded separately for documentary and (in your case) for tax reasons, are also reduced to a single balance for payment purposes by your stockbroker.

Dealing within the Account
Thus it is possible for you to buy and sell within the account, perhaps, if you wish, completely to sell all the shares you bought some days earlier, without having to pay the full principal. If by some chance your shares suddenly rise by a substantial amount, in response perhaps to an unexpected piece of good news, this may well be a perfectly sensible decision. It is not likely to happen to you often, but the market in any one period can demonstrate many large and sudden movements. It may well be that, in your judgment, the profit ought to be taken.

In this case, where your transaction has been extinguished over the account, you would still be sent two contract notes for the purchase and sale.

I don't need to point out that such a course of action might also, later on, prove to be hasty, since a share which rose during an account might rise even more in the subsequent period. Everything would depend on the circumstances.

I do need to point out, however, how speculative is the reverse of this transaction: that is, the selling of shares when you do not hold them, in the hope of buying them back at a lower price within the same account and therefore before you yourself have to deliver them. This is perfectly possible, because within the account the sequence of purchase and sales does not matter. It *is* done, by some professional speculators. But the risk of loss is open-ended, since you then *have* to buy the shares back: and *if* they rise, they can rise by any percentage!

Your share certificate

To revert to our simple transaction, however: the purchase of shares, as an investment holding. The date of the purchase, and the price, are those of the contract note. But, after settlement, you may not get your official 'share certificate' from the company whose shares you have bought for several weeks. Company secretaries are not equipped to process the turnover in their shareholders at the same speed as the Stock Exchange. You will get it, in due course, and you will own it, with all its rights, from the contract note date. In other words, the fact that you have not received the share certificate will not prevent dividends being routed to you (or, indeed, your selling the shares) before the certificate arrives.

5

Earnings and dividends – and how to measure them

How a company's earnings are calculated and how earnings and dividend criteria are used in expressing the rating of a share.

The most fundamental of all points about investment, underlying considerations of dividends received and the movements of share prices, are the profits made (or expected to be made) by the companies involved, and the growth in the wealth of companies arising out of these profits. The influences of general economic trends on company profits are many and varied. We are familiar with most of these from the news media.

But what exactly is a profit, how does it break down into the figures we see in the share quotations, and thus into a measurable quantity for investment purposes?

The essence of profit is, of course, simple. If a firm sells £5m of its products over the course of its financial year, and incurs total costs and charges of £4,615,000, it has £385,000 left at the year end. It has to pay corporation tax on this, which in the UK is currently 35 per cent. So our company has £250,000 after tax.

DISTRIBUTING THE PROFIT

Profit before tax	£385,000
Corporation tax, say	£135,000
Net profit after tax	£250,000
Net dividends on Ordinary shares	£125,000
Cover for dividends	$= \dfrac{£250,000}{£125,000} = 2.0$

It will normally distribute part of this profit in dividends to shareholders, the exact amount depending on how much cash it needs to retain in order to keep its operation intact: that is, to keep its plant or equipment up to date and to carry the stocks needed for continued trading.

Let us assume that the company decides to pay out half this net profit in dividends, a sum of £125,000.

The measurement of the profit and the dividend in terms of each share is again simple in principle. If the company's share capital consists of, say, £1m, divided into 1 million £1 shares, then the net profit will be 25p per share (£250,000 divided by 1m) and the dividend will be 12.5p net per share.

EARNINGS PER SHARE

Company share capital £1,000,000
(in £1 ordinary shares)   = 1,000,000 shares

Net profit after tax, all
attributable to Ordinary shares £250,000

$$\text{per share:} \quad \frac{£250,000}{1,000,000} = \begin{array}{c}\text{25p per share net}\\\text{earnings}\end{array}$$

Net ordinary dividend............ £125,000

$$\text{per share:} \quad \frac{£125,000}{1,000,000} = \begin{array}{c}\text{12.5 per share net}\\\text{dividend}\end{array}$$

If there is no other charge on the net profit, in the shape of payments to be made on a prior capital or to outside shareholders in subsidiary companies, the net profit is referred to as 'earnings', and the figure of 25p is known as 'earnings per share'. Bear in mind that, though this is technically all available for distribution to shareholders, the practical needs of the business, referred to previously, will in most cases demand some 'profit retention', as it is called, over and above, the amount set aside for replacement of existing plant (depreciation) which will have been knocked off before arriving at the pre-tax profit figure.

You can spot the relationship between the earnings per share and the net dividend per share in my example: it is twice. This relationship is known as 'dividend cover', (though in practice there are a number of slightly different ways of calculating this for reasons we need not go into at this point). If, for example, the dividend were only 2.5p, out of similar earnings per share, the cover would be 10 times. If the dividend had been 25p, it would be covered once. In fact, my chosen example is not too far from the normal average.

The 'Price/Earnings Ratio'
The value which the stockmarket may give to the company's shares depends on various factors, which we will look at later. For the moment, it is enough to point out that the market price of the shares is entirely independent of the 'par value'. So the above figures for earnings per share (eps) and dividend per share have to be turned into a measure of current value, related to share price.

Let us take the eps first; supposing that the shares' market price were 250p the 25p eps can be divided into this, giving a ratio of 10.0. This ratio is known as the Price Earnings Ratio, or PE, as it is abbreviated in the newspaper quotations. If the market price dropped to 300p, the PE ratio would become 12.0 (300 divided by 25). If the market price dropped to 200p, the PE ratio would fall to 8.0.

The Price Earnings Ratio is therefore, in principle, a very straightforward representation of the esteem in which the market holds the company concerned. The higher the PE ratio, the more popular the share – though there are exceptions which can throw this rule out.

How are dividends measured in relation to share prices? We could of course merely divide the dividend into the current market price of the share and call the result a 'Price Dividend Ratio'. But traditionally, because of the need for comparison with the returns given by all forms of investment and deposit income, we express the return as a yield. In other words, we divide the dividend by the current share price and express it as a percentage.

First, I must explain that UK companies pay dividends to their shareholders after deduction of basic rate income tax (currently 29 per cent). Shareholders who don't pay tax reclaim it, those who are higher taxpayers will eventually have to pay more, but in the form in which the dividend is paid out, it is net of basic rate.

Thus, our 12.5p dividend represents 71% of the full 'gross', or pre-tax, dividend. When a shareholder receives his dividend 'warrant', he can see the actual sum deducted in tax. But the gross dividend can easily be worked out by multiplying the net figure by 1.41 on your pocket calculator.

In the case of our example, this gives us a gross dividend of 17.6p (12.5p × 1.41).

'Grossing Up' the Dividends

Net dividend being 71% of 'gross' dividend
(i.e. after basic rate tax of 29%) 12.5p
Gross dividend = 12.5p × 1.41 = 17.6p

From this we can calculate the dividend yield of the shares which is normally expressed as a gross (before tax) figure. If the current share market price is 250p, the yield is 17.6p divided by 250p, all as a percentage. The answer on your calculator should be just over 7 per cent. Clearly, the higher the market price of the share rises, the lower becomes the yield. On a 300p market price, the yield will be just under 6 per cent (17.6 divided by 300p, all as a percentage). And if the price drops the yield will rise.

$$\text{Price Earnings Ratio} = \frac{\text{Market Price of share}}{\text{Net earnings per share}}$$

$$\text{e.g.} \quad \frac{250p}{25p} = 10.0 \text{ PE}$$

$$\text{Dividend yield} = \frac{\text{gross dividend per share}}{\text{Market price of share}} \times 100$$

$$\text{e.g.} \quad \frac{17.6p}{250p} \times 100 = 7.05\%$$

The reason why we don't use the net dividend (i.e. the 12.5p) to calculate yields is, as I mentioned before, to make proper comparisons with all other investment returns which are normally expressed before deducting tax. Since taxpayers come in all forms, from zero to 60 per cent, it makes sense to have a measure which is good for all.

6

Understanding company accounts

As a shareholder of any public company you will receive every year, as well as any dividends which might be paid, the report and accounts of the company. In the case of most of the well known quoted companies, this will contain a lot of information about the company's activities over the year and a statement by the chairman commenting on these. It is the most significant regular document on your investment which you will be well advised to look at carefully.

The most important items in the report are the two sets of figures detailing the profits for the year, and the balance sheet (that is, the state of the company's assets and liabilities) at the end of the period.

Most of the companies you are likely to invest in are really more than one company and pursue more than one type of business. It is very rare nowadays to find a large company which does not also own 'subsidiary' companies, which themselves have their own accounts.

However, company law obliges the company which 'holds' subsidiaries to group these together and present 'consolidated' accounts. This is what you receive as a shareholder of the group.

The profit and loss account

The first of these obligatory accounts is the 'profit and loss account' (P and L). The first item in this, starting at the top of the page, will usually be the figure for *sales*, or *turnover*. The second item is likely to be the profit earned on these sales after deducting the costs of raw materials, wages and salaries, and certain other items. Companies are not obliged to give breakdowns of raw material and wage costs as such, though some do.

Companies *are* obliged to detail other deductions, which they sometimes record in the 'P and L' account itself, or in notes which follow it. The first of these items is *depreciation*. Depreciation is not actually a cash item, spent by the company during the year. It is an amount set aside out of profits for the renewal of the company's 'fixed assets' (buildings, plant and equipment) based on estimates of the useful life of these assets.

The actual amount of cash *spent* on assets can be seen elsewhere, not in the 'P and L', and the reason for the depreciation figure is to represent the *need* for renewal of plant before reaching a 'true and fair' figure for profit.

Other deductions from profit after depreciation include the remuneration of directors and auditors. Directors' remuneration nowadays usually includes not only the fees for the actual directorships but also the salaries of directors who are also top executives.

Company borrowings – fixed and fluctuating

The item which can sometimes be of the greatest importance is that which details the interest paid over the year. The amount of borrowings varies greatly from company to company. Some companies may have to pay relatively large amounts in interest. Others may pay little or no interest, and yet others may have an excess of cash or other investments so that 'investment income' will appear as an item in the notes under the other contributions to profit.

Company borrowings fall into two main categories: overdrafts and other forms of bank loans; and fixed interest capital of the company.

The most essential point about bank lending is that interest rates on this will vary with the current bank base rates or other money rates.

Fixed interest capital, on the other hand, is issued in the same way as shares, is usually quoted on the Stock Exchange, and is fundamentally similar to gilt-edged stocks (though not necessarily as secure for an investor). It may be secured on property or other assets, or unsecured. But it has a fixed term before redemption and the interest rate is fixed also. Not much of this type of stock is issued nowadays, with interest rates so high, but many companies still have loan stocks of this kind, raised in earlier years.

Clearly the size of a company's interest bill is only important in relation to the profit before interest is paid. This relationship is often referred to as 'gearing'. It may be applied to the effect of interest charges on profit, as here; or it may be applied to the amount of the borrowing against the size of the company's assets (which will be dealt with later).

Profit before tax

After all these deductions, we have now reached the 'profit before tax', the figure we started at when looking at earnings in the last chapter. Companies in the UK are currently taxed at 35 per cent. Basic rate tax on company dividends, as we noted last time, is accounted for within this total of 35 per cent, however much of the profit is distributed to shareholders. So tax on UK company profits can never normally be more than this. However, there are many forms of tax allowance nowadays, and not many companies pay the full standard rate to the Revenue.

After tax, the profit figure remaining is sometimes subject to other deductions. If the company has subsidiaries where it does not hold all the shares, some of the profits of these subsidiaries will be due to the 'outside' shareholders or 'minorities' as they are called. The whole of the profit of these subsidiaries is in the 'consolidated' figures above the line, but the amount attributable to minorities is generally more conveniently taken out in one lump at the bottom.

The net profit

The remaining profit is usually called the 'net attributable profit' – 'net' because it is after tax and 'attributable' because it belongs to the shareholders of the company.

However, there may be a prior class of shareholders, to whom some dividend is due before the ordinary shareholders receive theirs. The most common of these prior classes is called the preference share. This is a fixed-dividend share. Most of the issues of such shares date back many years, and therefore the dividends on them usually represent very minor deductions from net profit.

After the payment due to any preference shareholders, we are left with the net earnings attributable to the ordinary shareholders (which, if you remember, we divide by the numbers of shares in issue to reach the figure of 'earnings per share').

From this figure, dividends paid or to be paid, for the year in question, are deducted. And anything left after this – the absolute bottom line – is known as 'retained profit' or 'profit retentions'.

Retentions are our link with the company's balance-sheet, which we will look at next: because this is the only bit of the operating profit for the year which actually increases the net assets that belong to shareholders.

GROUP PROFIT AND LOSS ACCOUNT

for the year ended 31st December, 1980

	Note	1980 £'000	1979 £'000
Turnover	1	883,906	836,265
Profit before interest	2	54,833	45,045
Interest payable	3	10,814	7,016
Profit before taxation		44,019	38,029
Taxation	4	10,362	8,478
Profit after taxation		33,657	29,551
Minority interests		(175)	(66)
Profit before extraordinary items		33,482	29,485
Extraordinary items	5	12,474	(2,827)
Profit attributable to Tarmac Limited	6	45,956	26,658
Dividends	7	9,226	7,605
Retained profit of the year	16	36,730	19,053
Earnings per ordinary share before extraordinary items	8	60.2p	53.4p

As an example of an actual profit and loss account I have taken that which Tarmac, the giant building and construction group, sent to its shareholders for the year 1980. You can see the items I have referred to, with one or two other features. First, you will notice that instead of giving a lot of minor detail, there are references to notes, which appear on subsequent pages of the report. For example, Note 2 would give some of the items deducted before the 'profit before interest' (for example, depreciation). Then Note 3 would give the interest split into its various categories – such as any fixed interest on loan stocks, or bank overdraft interest.

Second, the profit contains an item I haven't referred to. This is called 'extraordinary items', and it has a note to itself. Such items may be profits, on the sale of a factory for example, which are not part of normal trading and therefore need to be excluded from the 'earnings' figure. They may also include losses or payments which are likewise judged to be non-trading. This could include redundancy costs in closures of parts of the business. It is necessary to record such profits and losses but you can appreciate that since they are not repeatable they should not be part of the ongoing earnings figure.

FINDING YOUR WAY AROUND THE FIGURES IN A COMPANY BALANCE SHEET

A consolidated balance sheet is probably the second of the formal company accounts you will see in the annual report and accounts of the company in which you are a shareholder. Most of the companies whose shares you can buy on the Stock Exchange have 'subsidiary' companies whose individual accounts are merged into one for the purpose of reporting to the shareholder. As far as annual profits are concerned, these merged or consolidated figures are the only accounts presented. In the case of the balance sheet, we do get the balance sheet of the holding company presented, as well as the balance sheet, consolidated, of the 'group'. The latter is of course the most significant.

Assets and liabilities

What *is* a balance sheet? The name arises because, in the literal sense, it used to be presented as the balance between the assets of the company and its liabilities. The assets are its property, plant, equipment, stocks of goods and so on. The liabilities are what it owes to its bankers, to its suppliers, and unpaid bills of all kinds. The 'balance', that is the difference between assets and liabilities (which, in a viable company, will be a positive figure!) constitutes the 'net assets'.

Fixed assets

The presentation of the figures is nowadays often streamlined into a single column of figures, but the meaning of these remains the same. Taking a typical presentation, we see at the top of the page a figure for 'fixed assets'. This is the property, plant and equipment. We may also see just under this heading any other asset which is regarded as 'fixed'. Investments in other companies which are permanently held as part of trading policy are included here. So are investments in securities, such as gilt-edged stock.

In the notes to the balance sheet will be found numerous details of these items, including, for example, the categories of fixed asset, the depreciation which has over the years been charged against various items, and the new purchases of plant, equipment etc., made over the year. Detailed also in the fixed assets items will be 'goodwill' if there is any. Goodwill is the sum which does not represent 'tangible' assets – it is often there because of some past purchase, at a price higher than the strict value of the assets bought, or could represent patent rights the company owns and similar items. It is usually deducted when we are looking at what the company is worth to its shareholders.

Current assets and liabilities

Below fixed assets, we find two sets of figures: 'current assets' and 'current liabilities'. If fixed assets are regarded as the structure of the company, current assets represent the flow of business. They consist of: stocks and work-in-progress; debtors; and 'liquid assets'. The first item is self descriptive. The second, debtors, represents the money owing to the company by its customers. The third, liquid assets, may be cash in the bank, deposits, etc.

Current liabilities are the other side of this flow of business. They include 'creditors' (money which the company owes to its suppliers); bank overdrafts and other loans; tax owed to the Revenue; and other immediate items which usually include dividends not yet actually paid to shareholders.

If we take away current liabilities from current assets, we get a figure of 'net current assets'. Though there are cases where current liabilities are the larger figure, and where the subtraction will give net current liabilities, most well-run companies exhibit a fairly significant excess of current assets.

Net assets employed

The two forms of asset, 'fixed' and 'net current', together constitute the 'net assets' of the company. They are sometimes called the 'assets employed', because they are the physical, working constituents of the business.

What the balance sheet also shows is which part of this asset total belongs to shareholders, and which part to other claimants. Taking the latter first: there may be minority shareholders in group subsidiaries (referred to previously) whose share of the total assets has to appear separately. There may be mortgage, debenture or other loan stocks whose holders also have specific claims. And all other long-term financial liabilities will appear here, such as 'deferred tax'. This is tax which has been relieved by allowances but may have to be paid at an indefinite date; however, in some cases where it is unlikely the tax will ever become payable it may tend to be regarded as virtually belonging to the shareholders.

Net equity assets – capital and reserves

After all these claimants on the assets, we see the sum due to the shareholders. This is presented as two main figures: 'capital' and 'reserves'. The capital is simply the nominal or par value of all the shares. The reserves are, equally simply, all the rest. Reserves are divided up into various categories but these are basically mere book-keeping, except that certain classes of reserve cannot be distributed by way of dividend.

To take a simple example: if there are no 'minorities', no loan stocks, or other long-term items, then if a company's net assets are, say, £2.5m, then all this amount is due to shareholders. It doesn't matter for this purpose – though it might do in other contexts – whether the ordinary share capital is £0.5m, £1m or £2m (with 'reserves' of £2.0m, £1.5m or £0.5m respectively). The £2.5m is the figure of 'net equity assets'. When divided by the number of shares, we get a figure of 'net assets per share'.

It should be noted that if the company has preference shares as well as ordinary shares, these will be part of shareholders' funds. The nominal value of the preference shares has to be deducted from net assets before arriving at the amount attributable to ordinary shareholders, which is what we are concerned with when working out the 'net assets per share'.

GROUP BALANCE SHEET

at 31st December, 1980

		1980		1979	
Assets employed	Note	£'000	£'000	£'000	£'000
Fixed assets	9		140,354		122,193
Associated companies	10		6,066		8,291
Net current assets					
Stocks, stores and work in progress	11	112,963		86,997	
Debtors & long term contract work in progress	12	166,401		166,931	
Unlisted Investment		—		394	
Cash		5,131		9,192	
		284,495		263,514	
Creditors	13	199,398		203,015	
Short term loans and overdrafts	14	10,665		4,655	
		210,063		207,670	
			74,432		55,844
			220,852		186,328
Financed by					
Share capital	15		28,203		27,807
Reserves	16		132,649		97,773
Capital and reserves			160,852		125,580
Deferred taxation	17		3,321		17,707
Term loans	18		51,345		39,427
Deferred liabilities	19		3,964		2,876
Minority interests	20		1,370		738
			220,852		186,328

Tarmac's group balance sheet provides another illustration of how all these figures are represented. You can see how the main categories of asset are totted up in the right hand columns of each year reported. At the top, fixed assets, then 'associated companies', then net current assets, and finally the total (£220.8m) of 'assets employed'. You can see how this figure is recorded twice: first, looking at them as assets of the company, and second, looking at them as the total amount due to various parties.

The biggest part is due to the shareholders, in capital and reserves (the notes to these items may reveal a preference stock, which has a claim on part of these funds).

All other items beneath this are debts to somebody outside the company – either to the taxman, or to banks, or outside shareholders in subsidiary companies.

Thus, (if there are no preference shareholders) the amount of £160.8m is the figure which, divided by the number of ordinary shares, gives you the net assets per share.

7

Putting the figures to work

There are thousands of shares quoted on the Stock Exchange. Many hundreds of them represent sizeable companies. The back pages of the *Financial Times* list many of these, with their prices, yields and PE ratios. The *Investors Chronicle* regularly reviews their accounts, giving the essential statistics derived from their profits and balance sheets.

I have already outlined some of the most basis bits of investment arithmetic but I haven't yet touched on how these relate to real shares in the market. What do they mean in practice? How are the various measures of a company's profits, dividend and share price used as investment yardsticks?

You will recall what I said about a yield: that it represents the percentage return you receive on what you pay for a share, based usually on the latest annual dividend total; explained that 'cover' for the annual dividend represents how many times the cost of the dividend is covered by the net earnings of the company (though there are various methods of arriving at this); and explained that the PE (price/earnings) ratio represents the number of times that the net earnings per share goes into the share's market price.

Ratings on shares vary widely
Clearly, if Alpha Engineering's earnings and dividends have grown more than those of Beta Manufacturing over recent years, and if there were no signs of any halt to this trend, then investors will be prepared to take a lower current dividend yield on Alpha's shares than on Beta's, because they expect the dividend to rise faster in the future. They will also be prepared to put a higher 'multiple' on Alpha's current earnings that those of Beta (i.e. buy the shares on a higher PE ratio), again because they expect the earnings to grow more.

In the jargon of the stockmarket, Alpha's shares will be said to 'have a higher rating' than Beta's.

The differences in the ratings of individual shares result in very wide extremes in yield and PE ratio though, as you might expect, many shares fall into some sort of middle ground. There are, as I write, yields as low as 1 or 2 per cent, and PE ratios of 25 times and above. There are also yields as high as 13 per cent, and PE ratios as low as 2.0 or 3.0 times. In the middle, there are a lot of shares yielding 4 per cent, 5 per cent or 6 per cent. The FT/Actuaries average yield on 500 shares is about 4 per cent and the PE ratio about 13.0. This is not a true average but it gives a rough idea of it.

The rating of a share is not, of course, a scientific process. It is produced by the opinions of many investors, all focused at one point, in the market price. These opinions can be swayed by events both large and small, general economic trends and individual company experiences. The rating therefore changes from time to time, sometimes rapidly. It can be quite simply wrong, at any one time. And the price of a share can occasionally be swayed by technical market forces which have nothing to do with the basic arithmetic of the company or its prospects.

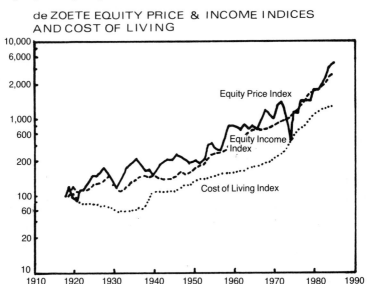

de ZOETE EQUITY PRICE & INCOME INDICES AND COST OF LIVING

The chart shows, over a very long period, how equity income has grown, and how capital values have followed this, but with considerable divergencies. As you will appreciate, where share prices have run ahead of income growth, yields will have narrowed, and vice versa. You may also note that the bull market of recent years has been justified by income growth. This is the market as an average, of course: and it is history. At any one date and with any one share, the future is uncertain, and expectation of growth will be firmer or weaker depending on the circumstances of the company.

For example, if the dividend is very well covered by the latest earnings, then there may be an acceptance of a lower yield now even though future earnings growth is not seen as above average. In this case there would have to be some confidence in the ability of the company to raise dividends even if earnings did not grow at the same rate.

Another factor which may influence the rating is the net asset value per share. If this is a lot higher than the share price in the market, then investors may be prepared to give the shares a rating above what otherwise would be their due. This is because the company might be taken over at some point, in which case its assets will figure in the price of a bid. Also, in some cases, these assets could be realised, or a new management could improve the return on them.

Naturally, the general trading background is an important criterion in assessing the merits of a share. The overall economic climate will affect all shares, but specific 'sectors' (different industries or groups of similar companies) will have different prospects. Certain sectors have had continuously higher growth than others and this is reflected in the performance of the shares concerned.

Of course, there will be periods of sharp downturn in profits, and threats of dividend cuts (as over the 1980-83 period) when some shares will fall, so that *historical* dividend yields rise to very high levels before the dividend cut is actually made. Then, when profits and dividends *have* fallen, the market may decide that a good recovery is likely, so the shares will rise to a point where the historical yield falls again and the PE ratio looks very high. This does not necessarily assume further steady growth afterwards but merely some restoration of previous profit levels.

Management – the vital factor

In the end, much of the variation in the rating of shares comes down to the quality of the company's management. This emerges in the arithmetic sooner or later.

Of course, management can change. One of the occasional rewards for the investor is to be able to pick up the signs of such change before the arithmetic shows them up. But that is another story.

Don't forget, either, that PE ratios, yields and the other investment yardsticks are only a guide to a share's rating. The accounting rules have now become so complex that different companies may present some of the items in their profit and loss accounts and balance sheets in different ways. Ratings worked out on the basis of these profits will not therefore always be comparable, one company with another.

And judging a company's rating is only one aspect of investment. You might, in fact, do better (in the short run at least) by buying the shares of a mediocre company when stockmarket prices were generally low than you would do by buying a far better growth prospect when the market as a whole was due for a fall.

8

Movements in markets

Share ratings are affected both by the company's own prospects and by market trends. Why do markets rise and fall?

The stockmarket assesses the shares of different companies, according to how investors as a whole view the prospects of growth in the earnings and dividends of each company, or the chances of any special event such as a takeover. The result of these assessments is a pattern of 'ratings', expressed in terms of yields and PE ratios.

Bull and bear markets

These ratings, these relative 'price tickets' attached to individual shares and groups of shares, are not static, as I pointed out. They may change for better or for worse. They are part of a general stockmarket picture which is subject to fluctuations; where these blend into a distinct trend upwards or downwards the terms 'bull' or 'bear' are used.

These terms derive from the original technical jargon of the market professionals. A 'bull' was a holder or buyer of stock taking the view that the price would rise. A 'bear' was a seller, on a view that the price would fall.

Why do markets rise and fall? There is a standard reply by market professionals to questions like this: there are more buyers than sellers for a rising market, and there are more sellers than buyers for a falling one.

This is of course a half jocular defence against the excessively detailed reasons and arguments that commentators like to come out with after any particularly noteworthy market movement. It happens, however, to be true. Bull and bear markets happen because of buying or selling pressure.

Just why and how this pressure arises and what explains its degree and its duration, are the questions which can't be answered, in any precise way. We can observe what has happened to stockmarkets over the last thirty years however, and draw some conclusions.

Post-war economic cycles

The first, factual, point is that stockmarkets from the early post-war years until 1974 moved up and down over a cycle of roughly four years or so, corresponding with the economic cycles of the period. They moved up in advance of the revival in activity and moved down before the recession in activity. In fact, stockmarkets always seem to anticipate events in the 'real' economy. Perhaps the most basic reason for this is that, when activity is low, the *need* for money in the economy is low – companies have cut back, people are more cautious. Thus, when the first stirrings of revival begin (for example, when the Government decides to pump more into the economy) this is felt first in the field of money. It goes towards reducing interest rates, because there will be, for a time, more credit than is actually needed. Where there is more of supply than demand, prices fall, and the 'price' of credit is the interest rate. At the same time, this expansion of money is helping to push up prices of all assets, including shares. As interest rates in other areas fall, investors are generally prepared to accept lower yields on ordinary shares as well.

This is why a falling trend in interest rates is associated with rises in stockmarkets (as well as in other assets, such as property).

After this phase of revival the economy will begin to absorb more money. At the peak of activity, perhaps long before any sign of 'real' downturn, the demands of real activity become too much. It may be that the Government will also decide to 'cool things off'. Money becomes more scarce. The stockmarket along with interest rates, begins to take the strain. Share prices begin to fall, the market is anticipating the downturn in the world outside.

This is the most fundamental reason why markets run ahead of the physical changes in the economy, and why in many cases there is no other sign of an upturn, or conversely a downturn.

Permutations of the cycle – high inflation

Of course, this is a vast over-simplification of the actual trends that markets and the economy have exhibited in recent years. The permutations have been considerable, and as a result each bull and bear market has shown different characteristics.

The biggest permutation was the development of high inflation after 1973. One reason is that inflation, in itself, is a 'consumer' of money. When reasonably constant, its effects may balance out. When it sharply accelerates it can depress markets by the same mechanism as a Government squeeze on credit. In 1974, this happened, whilst the Government was also mistakenly assisting the squeeze by its own policies.

In 1975, this process was sharply reversed. Inflation fell, and the Government also relaxed its policies. Since then, Governments have more or less coped with inflation (at least in terms of extreme movements), North Sea oil has entered the picture, and the result has been a much less clear pattern of so-called bull and bear markets. There has been a distinct rising trend, but punctuated by sharp falls from time to time.

Thus it has now become even more difficult to say, at any one time, that shares should be bought or sold, but if you look back at the chart of equity prices and income in the last chaper, you may conclude that the reduction of inflation has so far justified the long bull market of recent years.

It pays to act against 'the crowd'

There is still one maxim for individual investors which probably serves as well as it ever did, however. Whenever after a huge and hectic rise in shares, you read and hear universal enthusiasm for the stockmarket, wait before buying. The enthusiasm may evaporate and you will be able to buy lower down. By the same token, have the courage to start investing when the general atmosphere is full of gloom and uncertainty.

That advice applies to markets in general, and also to groups of shares in particular favour or disfavour.

It is, of course, much easier said than done: but it is the way that most successful investors have operated. Uncertainty is the biggest depressant of stock market prices. Because it is the hardest psychological barrier to crash it offers appropriate rewards. In recent years, the general movements of markets, and certainly the swings within different groups of shares, may well have been accentuated by the increasing size of the pension funds and other institutions which now own well over half of all the shares quoted on the stockmarket. The individual has more flexibility to act *against* the market in these circumstances.

In late 1974 there were almost no buyers of shares at all, certainly not in institutions. Great courage then would have been rewarded most handsomely.

9

Building a portfolio

Some basic rules of assembling a portfolio of investments are the same for everyone – but much depends on the individuals' circumstances and objectives

It should be obvious to any budding investor that simply popping your money into any share that takes your fancy is a pretty poor investment policy. To invest properly and responsibly, you will need to build up a 'portfolio', a number of shares in different sectors of the market, so that your risk in any one share or sector is diluted by the others.

The issues involved in portfolio building embrace a large part of investment theory and practice, but these are some of the basic principles.

The first and most important step is to work out clearly in your own mind exactly what you want out of your investment.

This starts with the most fundamental financial points referred to in earlier chapters, such as how much insurance you need, the size of your mortgage, the immediate liquid savings you need to maintain before you even begin to think about buying stocks and shares. And this of course will depend on your age, your job, your family's position and any other special circumstances.

Those circumstances will suggest the amount of 'free capital' you have and therefore the limits of your initial investment. They may also influence what sort of portfolio you should go for. For example, a young couple may need a lot of basic insurance and a large mortgage. They may not have so much to spare for investment, but may prefer a more adventurous investment policy with what they have. A couple near retirement will have more to spare, but may wish to pursue a safer strategy. In any case, you will have to decide what level of income from your investments you are prepared to go for in the initial stages (in other words, what the current yields on your shares must add up to) and what current income you are prepared to forgo in the expectation of a greater rise in income, and/or capital gain.

Spread of risk

The first question, on the amount you have available to invest, is related to the costs of dealing. You may recall what I said about these in an earlier chapter. The costs of dealing in any one share become higher if you are only able to buy in small quantities. And to achieve a minimum spread of risk you will need a minimum of ten well chosen shares. Thus if you have only a few hundred pounds then you will either have to go for a spread of risk by buying a unit trust or an investment trust, which will be buying a piece of an existing portfolio, or you will have to start with only one or two shares, and accept the higher risks. (This topic is referred to when discussing Personal Equity Plans on page 104.)

One way of adding to your investment portfolio at lower cost is to apply for new issues of shares when these are offered for sale: this can be fun, it can be rewarding; but it is haphazard, these issues are not frequent nowadays, and getting a full allotment of shares from an application is never certain. So this is not a 'starter' but an 'extra' which we will discuss at a later stage.

Choice of companies
Assuming that you have made the decision on the size of your available funds, how many separate companies should you have in your portfolio? I quoted ten as a minimum, and I think that most investment practitioners would regard this as low. It all depends on the choice of companies.

One factor which you, as a small investor, don't have to worry about as much as the institutions do is 'marketability', that is, the ability to buy or sell at the going price in significant amounts of stock. Big investment funds have to reckon with this problem, which is one important reason why institutional portfolios have to have a much wider spread than this. You can afford to be more concentrated, in this respect, though in some companies where shares change hands very infrequently you still need to pick your moment and make sure you do not inadvertently push the price up against yourself.

You also do not have to hold more than one share in any one sector, provided that it is reasonably representative. In other words, you need only hold one brewery share, one share of the Big Four banks, one share in the food manufacturing business, one retail store, and so on.

You don't need every sector
Nor do you have to hold a share in every possible sector, provided that you make sure that you have the maximum diversity in the sectors. For example, you will need some share in each of the major areas of retail, manufacturing, financial services and commodities. Somewhere, either as an addition to or as a component of one of the other shares, you will want some overseas element. Expanding from this base, you may then decide on two or three areas of retailing, a bank and an insurance company, three or four manufacturers in different industrial products, an oil company and a mining company.

These are the sort of steps necessary to get enough 'diversification'. The 'safer' you want your portfolio to be, the more widely spread it should be. If you want to be more venturesome, then you will want to concentrate on sectors which are expected to give more growth. In this case, the timing of your purchases (see the previous chapter on market movements) will be more important, as will be the precise shares you select.

In share selection, the obvious aim is to buy the *best value* share in each sector. There always are companies which are *better* than the rest: unfortunately, they are usually highly rated and will not necessarily be *best value*. So, after doing all your homework on a short list of shares, you must decide if you will go for medium rated companies and hope to see them get better (in every sense) or accept the verdict of the market and hope for the higher growth that goes with the higher price tag.

But, in any case, don't be in a hurry. If you pick up your portfolio one share at a time, thinking about it as you go, you will make fewer mistakes.

Moreover, you will be reducing your exposure to any particular market period, which is no bad thing, unless you are convinced that such-and-such a time is absolutely right. In which case, please let me know, will you?

COMPANIES AND THEIR CHARACTERISTICS

The most important characteristic of any share to an investor is whether the company in question is likely to grow fast or not, whether it is relatively safe or not; as it affects the share price and the future income. These characteristics vary between companies, even in the same trades and industries. Nevertheless, there are certain characteristics which are more common in one sector rather than another, so we will begin by looking at shares from this point of view.

Form of activity

Perhaps I should use the phrase 'form of activity' rather than the word 'sector' here. The so-called sectors are classified in the Financial Times Actuaries indices, to be found near the back of the *Financial Times*. There are several groups and a large number of sub-groups. The FT also classifies its quoted shares, on the back pages, in a different manner, according to a revised version of the original Stock Exchange method of classification. However, I would like to define certain more fundamental characteristics. For convenience, I will group companies according to whether they are in the business of making things, distributing things, providing services of many kinds or producing basic raw materials (the resource stocks).

Companies which make things

The first and most obvious fact to emerge from the sector classifications is that a large proportion of companies are in the business of 'making' something or other. It may be a product which sells direct to the consumer (and here the dividing lines between 'making' and 'distributing' become blurred, as in the case with the brewery companies). It may be a product with a longer life span (a refrigerator or a domestic appliance, say) but where the consumer is again the customer. Or it may be a product for which other companies are the customers (a metal forging, say) and they in turn incorporate it into a product such as a car which is eventually sold to the consumer. It may be an item of plant (a machine tool, for example), which other companies in turn use to produce their own products.

The characteristics of a share in what might broadly be called the 'manufacturing' sector can therefore be affected by a wide variety of factors. Does the company sell direct (or almost direct) to the public? Is its product one for which there will always be a demand (though not necessarily a rapidly growing one) like beer or bread? Does it make products which can be sold abroad or where overseas manufacturers can compete with it on its home base? Does it supply an industry which itself is in decline? Is it most dependent at any one time on the levels of capital investment or of consumer demand in the economy? These and many other factors have to be taken into account before even considering the position of an individual company within its particular business.

Service or distribution companies

If Britain's traditional industries have been in decline, many of the non-manufacturing businesses have been moving the other way. These range from international 'service' business such as insurance or banking which can be important earners of foreign currency, to the other types of 'service' business such as retailing or cleaning which are almost dependent on the domestic market. Napoleon's description of the British as a nation of shopkeepers remains true today and some of the greatest stockmarket success stories have been in the field of retailing. It is not necessarily that the total market has expanded, but new entrepreneurs have discovered more efficient and more profitable methods of attracting the consumer.

'Resource' companies

Finally, within our very broad categorisation of businesses we have to mention the 'resource' stocks: the companies which mine, drill or plough for the basic raw materials without which little else can function. Oil has come closer to home with the North Sea finds and has enormously increased its importance to the UK economy. Many of the other resource stocks, in particular the mining and plantation companies, may operate largely abroad, though the shares of many of them are quoted in London.

SOME EXAMPLES OF THE BROAD CATEGORIES OF ACTIVITY GIVING 'DIVERSIFICATION' OF INVESTMENT*

Manufacturing	Services	Distribution	Commodities and resources
building materials	financial services (banks, insurance etc.)	food retail	oil & gas
Mechanical engineering		drink retail	mining
electrical & electronic engineering	design & construction	clothing	other raw materials (e.g. rubber)
metal manufacturing	agencies (advertising, marketing)	mail order	food
motor components	cleaning	electrical & electronic products	
chemicals	office equipment services (data processing)	stores	
paper & packaging		industrial products (coal, oil, chemicals)	
textiles	shipping & transport		
food & tobacco	leisure		

* Many companies are in several forms of activity. Many of the industries in the list are intrinsically in more than one activity (e.g. brewing is both manufacture and distribution, so are food and tobacco).

In the next chapters we will be looking at the characteristics of some of the different types of companies within these broad divisions. But right at the outset a number of points are clear:
● Real growth is hard to find, and perhaps hardest of all to find within the traditional manufacturing business. Many a company which has ostensibly increased its profits most years may in practice have done no more than keep

pace with inflation. It is not expanding in any real sense, but the money value of what it sells has risen as the purchasing value of that money has declined. This in itself is not to be sneezed at by an investor, provided dividends have kept pace. As long as the company is being realistic about what it sets aside each year to replace its plant and equipment, the shares provide an inflation hedge of a kind.

● The amount of money tied up in plant and equipment – the 'fixed assets' of the company – will vary enormously between different types of business. At the one extreme there is the property investment company whose assets are (readily saleable) buildings which are probably increasing in value; but these companies often show a comparatively low income return from these assets. In the middle would come many manufacturing companies, which need large scale investment in (less saleable) plant and machinery to produce their goods and – generally – fairly large amounts of cash to finance their working capital requirements. Lower down the scale would come the retailing businesses, which may happen to own their shop and warehouse premises but do not need to do so. In theory a retailer can set up with a rented shop and a small amount of capital to cover his stocks and his debtors. Some of the more efficient retailers, in practice, find their need for working capital diminishes as their business grows – simply because they turn their goods round so fast that they get the cash from the customer before they have to pay the supplier for them.

At the other end of the scale, certain types of service company need little if anything in the way of fixed assets. The value of, say, an advertising agency can be almost entirely in 'goodwill': the intangible assets such as the expertise of its staff on which the success of its business depends.

● A company may be in a business where its profits show a fairly stable trend, or it may be in one where they fluctuate quite widely from year to year. If the company is highly geared – in other words, if the amount of borrowed money in the business is large relative to the amount of shareholders' money – these profit swings will be accentuated.

All of these factors will need to be borne in mind when we come to examine the different types of company – and their investment characteristics – in detail.

10

Manufacturing companies: the problem areas

Manufacturing companies are by far the most diverse category of share. They cover everything from makers of power generating equipment to makers of mint humbugs. And any balanced portfolio of shares is bound to include a number of manufacturing companies.

Given the diversity of manufacturing industry (and given the fact that most larger companies actually undertake a number of different operations under the umbrella of the group name) it is more than usually difficult to generalise about the investment characteristics of manufacturers. But let's start with a few points which will help us understand what is happening in British industry today (though don't assume they apply to every single manufacturer):

● By and large, making something requires fairly heavy investment in plant and equipment or heavy investment in labour, or both. A commodity dealer can generate a turnover of millions with few tools beyond a telephone. A manufacturer cannot.

● The plant and equipment of a manufacturing concern is likely to be costly. But it wears out or becomes obsolete, and it may have very little resale value if the original owner finds he cannot use it to produce goods at a profit.

● Restrictive practices by trade unions and inertia on the part of managements (blame which you like – or both) have often meant that the British manufacturer has produced goods less efficiently than his foreign counterpart. While sterling was weakening against other currencies he could often get away with it and still sell his goods in competition with foreigners. When Britain became an oil producer and sterling strengthened, the position of many manufacturers looked much less promising. As sterling dropped from its 'petro-currency' peak the position for manufacturers improved again.

● Britain's rate of inflation – far above the average for the developed countries until recently – has tended to disguise the true profit trend of many manufacturing concerns. This is for two main reasons. Companies have not made sufficiently large provision each year for the costs of replacing their plant and equipment at tomorrow's higher prices before arriving at a published 'profit' figure. Neither have they allowed for the fact that much of their profit may have been earned by selling at today's prices goods manufactured from materials bought at last year's lower prices. 'Inflation-adjusted' profit figures, which seek to allow for these two factors amongst others, are becoming obligatory for quoted companies, at least as a

* See glossary under 'Current Cost Accounting'.

supplement to the traditional form of accounts*. Without going into detail on this, it is evident that the inflation adjusted – i.e. 'real' – profits of manufacturers were generally well below the profits the accounts have traditionally shown.

Now after reading this catalogue of problems you might be forgiven for thinking the investor should steer clear of the manufacturing sector altogether. This is not, of course, the case. But it is true to say that some of the basic manufacturing industries in Britain have been in relative decline for many years, that the decline was sometimes masked by the factors we have mentioned, but that it was thrown into sharp relief by a combination of high sterling, high interest rates and the policies followed by the Conservative Government which came to power in 1979.

Restructuring in 1980 and 1981
These factors culminated in an unprecedented decline in industrial production from 1980 to 1983 and an unprecedented restructuring of many industrial operations. The worst affected firms have been those in steel-making, textile production, basic chemicals production and in engineering firms supplying the motor industry. We'll look at these first, moving on to the more prosperous manufacturing sectors afterwards.

The rise of 'basic' industries such as steel and textiles in the third world, and the special challenge of Japan in the motor industry, have affected all the Western industrial nations, but Britain possibly worst. Steel (mainly nationalised, but with some private sector firms), basic chemicals and the most basic textile operations are all 'capital intensive'. Expensive plant needs a big throughput to cover its costs. In Britain in 1980, with sterling riding high, this was simply not available. Companies such as GKN in steel and engineering, ICI in chemicals and Courtaulds in fibres were forced to close down plant. It is not simply that the plant often has to be written off. There are usually associated costs of redundancy payments to the workers who lose their jobs.

The motor industry is different in many respects from these others. Its products are not 'basic'. They are sold ultimately to individual consumers and therefore can, with the right management, be promoted profitably even when there are many difficulties such as rises in raw material costs and rises in the currency.

But the British motor manufacturers have generally failed to match the production efficiency and production scale of the best of the overseas manufacturers, who have gained a competitive advantage. And this has seriously affected the fortunes of the myriad of engineering companies which supply components that ultimately end up in the motor vehicle. The leading companies have made strenuous efforts to develop their products for sale overseas, both by exporting and by local manufacture. They have sought to diversify outside the motor industry. The household names such as Lucas, AE and GKN have a wealth of accumulated engineering expertise that should ensure them a continuing if changing place in the world's markets. But the transition is costly and slow.

The stockmarket mirrored the misfortunes of these sectors we have identified as worst affected by the trends of 1980-82. Share prices fell sharply.

Because of the loss of profit already sustained, these companies' cash diminished, and/or their borrowings increased. Thus their 'gearing' (borrow-

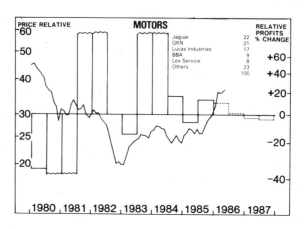

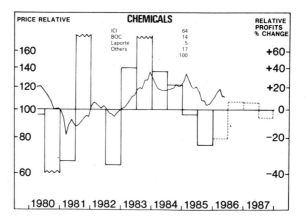

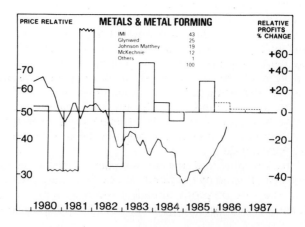

ings against shareholders funds) increased, though this still varied widely between companies. In most cases, their share prices were far below the 'net asset values' of the shares, though, as we have pointed out, the assets involved may not be saleable, at least not at their book value at that point.

However, when these conditions prevail in the stockmarket, it pays to look carefully at the shares concerned because at some stage there may be a substantial recovery in many of them, as proved to be the case in a subsequent period. These depressed companies provided some of the best subsequent share performances in the period after 1983.

The graphs, prepared by the stockbrokers Phillips & Drew, show three out of the many manufacturing sectors which were hit so badly and have since recovered. Each line on the graphs shows the performance of the Financial Times Actuaries Index for that sector (i.e. an average of the share prices of the major stocks). The line is not the actual performance, but that relative to the All Share Index. Thus, the motors average shows a fall from 45 in 1979 to 20 in 1982, which means that these shares had dropped by 25 per cent in relation to the market as a whole. Note, however, that from then until 1986 they did better than the market by 17 per cent (from 20 to 37).

The bars on the chart are Phillips & Drew's calculations of the way in which the sector's profits have changed, but again relative to total industrial profits.

In broad outline these charts show depression and recovery. They also show how the shares' movements anticipate events in the shape of rising profits.

THE MORE STABLE MANUFACTURING SECTORS

Low growth may not matter if there is no heavy capital outlay necessary in advance; or if, despite a heavy capital requirement, the growth can be controlled or predictable. This stability of growth is more easily obtained where competition is limited to the UK or, better still, to the locality of the firm.

The latter conditions are usually present in the building materials industry. Here, Britain has produced a number of large and successful companies. Cement production is expensive of capital, and is a 'process' industry (continuous production of a standard substance). However, since demand is relatively predictable, and anything but local competition is excluded by the costs of transport, it can be (and usually is) very profitable. These firms have performed reasonably against the average.

As with many other industries, local success often breeds expertise which can be exploited elsewhere; and a number of big British cement manufacturers have plants abroad, notably Blue Circle, among the largest of UK companies.

Within this field (that is, very high volume, capital-intensive processes) the most interest example is Pilkington Bros. This company has been able, for many years, to exploit its invention of the 'float glass' process in the UK, thus ensuring the relatively controllable growth to justify the massive capital expenditure involved. It also reduced the risk of overseas expansion by licensing other companies to produce float glass. By good management, the risks have been reduced as much as possible without sacrificing the aim of continous growth. And the reward over a period of years has been very high profitability, though in 1981/83 it was not able to avoid the effects of the recession in the UK and elsewhere.

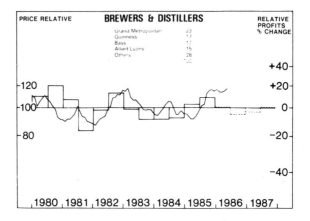

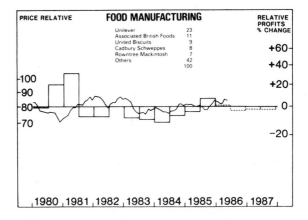

There are other areas of process manufacturing where the reliability of demand is an important factor in the build-up of profitable high-volume production. Brewing is certainly the biggest example, and the bread and confectionery industries provide another. In these cases, there is also a chain of distribution involved to the final consumer, so the stability of these industries is notable, as is shown by the relative performance charts. Very successful cases in these industries, where management has picked out the right trend in consumer taste and preference, are very profitable indeed. The unsuccessful cases can be very disappointing investments, over long periods. But they offer, when the prices of the shares concerned are on very low ratings, a combination of low risk and some possibility of further revival. A case in point with Ranks Hovis McDougall, which got to grips with its problems of too many outdated milling and baking plants and then performed very well.

Engineering

The engineering industries, which is what most people think of when the word 'industry' is used, vary considerably in their use of capital. The big 'engineering contractors' may manufacture large items of industrial plant themselves, but their special skills are in the construction of plant and the organisation of the whole process. In this, they use other people's capital, by means of advance deposits and 'progress payments'. This area is a special British skill. But the cycle of activity can lead to big downturns, as well as sharp recoveries.

The 'heavy' manufacturers, those who build power generation equipment, for example, also use the customers' capital during the long cycle of production. Even so, they need to be especially careful of their own finances. They are particularly exposed to unforeseen changes in the rate of inflation and overseas currency prices because of this lag between order and delivery.

Therefore, the profit margin on each item has to be high. Technical standards are the hallmark of this sector, and it is a tough world for the companies involved, particularly if, as in the UK in recent years, the growth in power generation demand (from the Government) has been low.

Electronics

Of course, there have been some areas of growth visible in UK manufacturing. These tend to be in specialised areas, and/or the exploitation of overseas trends. One of these is telecommunications. Most aspects of electronics have grown in the UK, even though the ultimate consumer electronic industries are centred elsewhere. Defence, as it is called, has also been a growth area in the UK, and is another particular British speciality worldwide. Defence nowadays is largely electronics of a specialised kind and UK firms have always been good at specialised, highly research-oriented work. The giant companies in this area include GEC, Plessey and Racal. Of course, the giant of telecommunications is British Telecom. But one should not view British Telecom principally as a manufacturer. It is a 'service company' of a very specialised kind.

Electronics was, in fact, not a good sector to have been in from 1983 to 1986, as problems developed in various fields. But it still contains examples of the fastest potential growth areas in manufacturing.

Catching them while they are small

We've been talking here about the characteristics of major companies. Every investor's dream, of course, is to spot one of the growth companies of the future while it is still small and before the share price reflects the potential.

There *are* small companies in the manufacturing sector in the UK which, by spotting a specialist gap in the market place and exploiting it with the strength of good management, may offer these characteristics. But they are rare. Opportunities for this sort of operation are more often found in retailing and service companies, which we will be examining next.

11

Success among the retailers

It's relatively easy to set up shop, but profit depends on much more than products

Retailing has thrown up a disproportionate number of success stories in the stockmarket over the years. There are many reasons for this. Most retail operations need comparatively little fixed capital, either to start up or indeed to maintain the business. Furthermore, by owing money to their suppliers for stock which is sold before payment is due, many kinds of fast-selling retail businesses can avoid the need for current bank finance.

To firms of this kind, the inflationary conditions in Britain over the past twenty years or so have been favourable. Inflation, so long is it doesn't get too far out of control, is basically kind to businesses which don't have to *make* the goods, but merely transfer them with the appropriate sales mark-up to the final customer.

Intense competition
This is not to say that Britain is a paradise for retailers. Indeed, the very characteristics I have outlined create an intensely competitive environment. Anyone can start up, challenge his rivals, and succeed (if he has identified the right area, the right products, pursues the right strategy, manages the shops efficiently etc). Or he can fail (by not doing these right things). There have been plenty of failures amongst newcomers, and plenty of disappointment and decline in established businesses.

Nevertheless, given the right dynamism and efficiency, the nature of retailing in the UK has made it possible for many entrepreneurs to establish themselves fairly quickly, and for larger companies with good management to 'create' growth.

This growth has been achieved in many cases at the expense of others, particularly in food retailing, where annual growth in the country as a whole is pretty low, but where the supermarkets have displaced the small grocery stores and the older chain groceries of the 'Co-op'. But growth has also arisen from entirely new specialised markets, such as those in electrical and electronic goods or in 'do-it-yourself' products.

The breakdown of resale price maintenance
One of the most important developments for this type of retailing, and the thing which has distinguished Britain from Europe over most of the past few years, was the enforced abandonment of resale price maintenance. This took several years, during the early sixties, to phase in over the whole retail range.

But it was nonetheless a revolution. It broke the power of the manufacturer in Britain over his outlets. It made it easy for big food and 'consumer durable' chains to exert their buying power where they wanted to, then to cut their selling prices as much as they wished, and thus to achieve a powerful engine for fast sales growth at the expense of their smaller or less efficient rivals.

It is also fair to say that it did encourage efficiency in retailing, and probably increased the *overall* growth rate of sales for quite some time.

The formula, in the best groups, produces a high return on the capital. If it can be coupled to continuous physical expansion, into new sites and by the enlargement of existing sites, then significant 'real' growth can be maintained. There is seldom much need for equity finance in all this, so existing shareholders get all the rewards.

The shares of these successful fast growing companies have of course had their fluctuations, some them dramatic (as in 1974) but the overall result to date has been markedly better than for the stockmarket as a whole. The chart of the relative performance of the food retail sector illustrates this point.

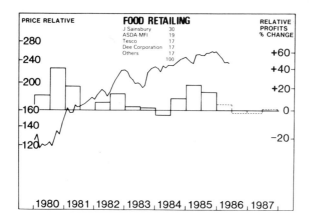

One of the formulae for success, exhibited by all the leaders, has been specialisation, the concentration on one range of products, one style of service, or one sector of custom. In food, this is exemplified by Kwik Save (ruthless price cutting on a strictly limited food range), by ASDA (somewhat higher prices with a full supermarket range of products) and Sainsbury's (prices even higher but more emphasis on style and type of customer). In the 'multiple stores', the aims and the styles of Marks and Spencer need no description from me. Other leaders, in other areas, such as Dixons, all show either one emphasis of product or one coherent approach to the customer.

In an earlier era, socially and financially, there were other successful growth formulae. The great department stores, which arose out of cheap mass transport to city centres, when the advantage of all things under one roof was not offset by high labour costs and high interest rates, are the products of *their* time. In more recent years, they have been fighting against the newer trends. They have responded by closedown, merger and takeover, by reshaping their style, by creating specialised areas within their stores. But none of them has had an easy time. The decline of their basic profitability, though not spectacular compared with some manufacturing firms, left their share ratings considerably lower than the first group discussed. It follows that their share prices are usually lower, in some cases very much lower, than their net asset values per share, values which are based *inter alia* on prime city centre or High Street freehold property. These values have attracted takeover bids from time to time, notably those for Debenhams and House of Fraser.

In the 'multiple store' field, whereas we see Marks and Spencer with above-average performance at one end, we also had Woolworth at the other. Woolworth's formulae was a winner in its day, and its physical growth brought it to giant size in terms of the competition. But the formulae is no longer appropriate, its very size makes adaptation difficult, and it is no longer very profitable. On the other hand, its very saleable assets are worth far more than the share price which was why, it was eventually taken over and is now being partly revamped and partly sold-off.

In the supermarket field, Tesco is an example of a once highly successful supermarket group, one of the first, which grew to be the giant of the sector but which went through a bad patch in the late 70s as profitability declined.

Whatever the reasons for this, it certainly demonstrates that there is nothing automatic about real growth of profits. Thus the task of the investor is to watch for the budding new growth areas before they have got too far off the ground. These may be in products, or techniques of selling, or the identification of new sectors of demand. 'Real' growth will have to involve the last two – it is not good enough to have a better mousetrap if you can't get the people in to buy it, or if you haven't worked out who needs mousetraps!

PROVIDING SERVICE AT A PROFIT

Service companies, like retailers, have often enjoyed considerable success in Britain, even at a time of minimal economic growth. In commercial terms, a service is that element of assistance provided by an individual or a firm to the customer or client, which does not involve any goods or materials. In terms of capital resources, therefore, it is furthest down the line from manufacturing or retail. Many services can be provided with the minimum of capital, either for equipment or materials.

Most of the 'capital' involved in providing a service is intangible, consisting of just the training and experience which is necessary. The higher and more specific the level of skill, the more expensive it has been, and the more likely it is that some firm (as distinct from the educational system!) has paid for it. But it doesn't belong to the firm. It walks in, and out, with the individual who has it. Providing a service can thus be very profitable. The right specialisation and the right strategy can create real growth. However, the world is full of mistakes in both these things. The swings of customer preference can kill a growth trend in demand. If the skills involved are rudimentary, competition will be easy. If they are on a high level, they will be costly to develop and maintain. Good management, as always, is necessary to handle both these innate difficulties.

Service – an element of all business

All businesses have an element of service. In fact, it may be said of many engineering businesses that the service element is a vital part of their success and profitability.

The big engineering contractors are the extreme case of this. Much of their 'capital' is in their design teams. The most successful building firms are those whose 'service' element is strongest, as represented in their planning departments and their site management.

The purest examples of service companies are the advertising and other agencies. Successful examples of these are very much the product of personal talent, drive, but also of 'management' – the right system for the encouragement of talents in others. Saatchi and Saatchi in advertising is the current most prominent example – with a remarkable growth record, but, as you might expect, a very high share rating.

Employment bureaux are another pure form: so is auctioneering, where in art (Sothebys and Christies) and motor cars (British Car Auctions) the leaders have grown enormously. In these cases, too large an organisation can be caught out by a decline in customer demand.

The new computer businesses
Further examples are to be found in the computer businesses which have arisen in recent years. The manufacture of 'hardware' in computing is, of course, the basis of the electronics firms who turn out the microchips and other devices. But the development of software is not manufacturing in the old sense, but the application of skill – in effect, a sort of service, though a very high-powered variety of it. The right strategy in such firms can maintain growth – genuine growth – despite the competition. But the pitfalls, as in any growth field, are correspondingly dangerous.

The TV companies
The commercial TV companies are a mature, but still 'high-powered' service sector. The late Lord Thomson described this business as a licence to print money, and that proved to be an accurate if crude assessment of the first phase of commercial television. The point Lord Thomson appreciated was that each company had relatively low capital needs, an enormous potential market, and no competitors in its own area. Lack of competition has always been good for the investors in any enterprise, whether earned (as by Xerox and Polaroid through the design of patents and know-how) or granted (as by the medieval monarchs to their favourite trades, and by the IBA to the TV companies).

However, the IBA was capable of revising its licences, and altering the conditions of them. Thus the TV companies have not had it entirely their own way and because of the uncertainties over future TV policy they are not highly rated. Some have expanded greatly into other activities of which some have succeeded (such as Granada in its TV rental business) and some did not (such as Associated Communications, in its blockbuster film-making).

If these are high-powered services, there are plenty of 'low-powered' ones around. The travel business is a prominent example, highly specialised in the 'package' form, with periods of high growth, but very competitive and subject to large risks.

Another, more humdrum example, less 'pure' because it involves capital equipment of various sorts, is the laundry and cleaning business. This has had two growth phases. The first was in the era of low-cost labour and no domestic washing machinery, when the big laundry chains arose. Then followed decline. The second growth phase, achieved after much heartache and reorganisation, has been in *industrial* laundry and cleaning, still highly competitive but profitable and growing.

Hotels and catering

The biggest of the service industries, where the investment character is flavoured by the property angle, is the hotel and catering business. This is of the 'low-key' variety, but where experience and flair in management is mixed with property expertise in the most successful examples, because hotels *do* involve large capital outlay. The two giants of the industry, THF Group and Grand Metropolitan, have been created by skills in takeover as much as in management. Both now have wide interests outside hotels, Grand Met notably in brewing and milk.

In more recent success stories, the managements of companies such as Norfolk Capital and Reo Stakis have exercised the same acquisitive skills. Hotels are *not* highly profitable in terms of return on capital employed but do generate a large turnover with minimum stocks, and in an inflationary era their premises tend to appreciate in value. Because the pure hotel operation provides a stable base for other activities, many hotel groups are also in the 'entertainment' field. Some have gone into one of the British specialities – gambling, the ultimate service business!

12

Banking and insurance shares

BANKS AND DISCOUNT HOUSES

There are four main types of quoted company whose business is in lending money in one form or another. The first, and by far the biggest as a group, are the clearing banks and other commercial banks.

Secondly, there are the so-called merchant banks, whose activities are varied and by no means confined to lending. Thirdly, there are the hire-purchase or finance houses, which have now virtually all been taken over by the clearing banks. Fourthly, there are discount houses, which are highly specialised companies which lend within the money markets used by the Government and other banks.

The clearing banks

The most readily observable and understandable of these groups by the average investor are the commercial banks, and particularly the 'big four', Barclays, Lloyds, Midland and National Westminster. These four are individually amongst the very biggest of UK companies, and between them are responsible for most of the everyday lending to individuals and to industry in England and Wales. They are known as 'clearing banks' because they share the London-based cheque clearing operation which sorts out all cheque transactions daily and settles up between the members.

As well as the big four, there are two Scottish banks which are still separately quoted companies. There are two Irish banks, both very much linked to London but now technically foreign. There is also the TSB, which has risen from its lowly savings origins to be challenger to the others. And there is Standard Chartered the last remnant of the old imperial and colonial banks.

Shares of the big four, though their earnings and dividends have grown quite satisfactorily over the years, have performed relatively badly in the years since 1973, even though their profit growth has been above average. This is partly because investors are worried about how these giant organisations, with their huge and costly branch networks, are going to cope with the continuing problems of inflation and fluctuating interest rates in the years ahead. A large proportion of their UK deposits (i.e. our money) are on current account, paying no interest to the customer (though the costs of the banking service have to be covered). When interest rates shoot up, the banks' lending rates also rise but they only have to pay interest out on

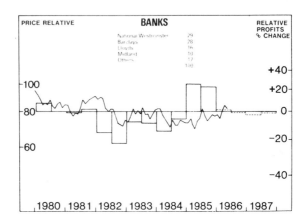

their 'deposit accounts'. So the effect on profits is disproportionate. But the effect works both ways, up and down. Meanwhile, the costs of providing the banking services have risen and are rising. So what happens when the interest rate advantage of the current account system becomes overwhelmed by the servicing costs of the branches?

The banks are aware of this, and are doing their best to cut costs at home. They have also expanded and are still expanding into other spheres.

Investors have other worries about banks, which have varied from time to time. Most of these worries boil down to periodic fears that they will need to come to the market to raise cash via rights issues. The shares currently reflect these worries and their ratings (yields and PE ratios) are amongst the lowest of the market sectors despite their good dividend records. As such, they can be said to be fairly safe investments, with the chance of capital growth dependent on a decline in inflation and a more settled period for interest rates.

The merchant banks

Merchant banks are quite different. They arose originally out of the enormous British interest in trade, and its need of finance. They have developed in many ways since then, and each varies widely in its range of activities. These include investment management, precious metal dealing, and corporate finance (which covers all forms of help to companies in raising money as well as advice in such matters as takeover bids). But they all, in greater or lesser degree, maintain their actual lending to companies linked to trade finance, in the form of 'acceptances' which are a kind of promissory note, given the seal of approval by the bank, so that the exporter or importer is not out of the money whilst the goods in question are in transit. Some of them have gone into direct Stock Exchange activity through broking and market making.

The shares of merchant banks have always tended to fluctuate in more extreme fashion than most, and in the 1970s were disappointing investments. They may be expected to do very well when interest rates fall and stockmarket activity rises, because so much of their business is linked to this. One of the disadvantages to an outside investor is that these banks are not obliged to disclose their banking profits fully. By permission of the Bank of England, they make undisclosed provisions before publishing their profit figures.

The discount houses

Finally, there are the discount houses. These are a select group of companies, most of them quite small in terms of share capitalisation, whose main function used to be helping the Bank of England in its task of smoothing out the flows of funds (lending and borrowing) between the Government and the financial community (that is, ultimately, people and companies). The Government, for example, may be taking a lot of money out of the 'system' in tax at a certain period. Or it may need money to cover a shortfall, and thus wish to borrow on short term to cover this. The discount houses operate between the Bank of England and the banking community as a channel for this short term in-and-out flow. They earn their money on the difference (established by their privileged position) between their borrowing costs from the banks and their receipts from lending-on to the Government.

Over the years the discount houses have greatly widened their operations in money markets, dealing in 'bills' of different kinds, for trade and commerce. The common feature is of huge turnover, with narrow margins for the discount house go-between.

Such a background sounds unpromising. Yet, although for many years the shares have had a lowly rating, dividends have grown and the total return for those interested in income has been very satisfactory. Some discount houses have been taken over by both British and overseas financial groups because their expertise is valued in the new Stock Exchange environment. Others have decided that their skills in making markets in money can be extended to the much wider gilt-edged and bond market activity open to them.

INSURANCE COMPANIES, ASSURANCE COMPANIES AND BROKERS

Like many other financial services, 'general' insurance is one of the great British specialities. The term 'general' insurance embraces the insurance of all types of risk (household, aviation, marine etc.) other than life assurance.

Historically, a very large proportion of the overall business of the general insurance companies has been in North America and this is still about as big as UK business, taking the industry as a whole. In the case of the two biggest companies, Royal Insurance and Commercial Union, North America is the single largest area of operation.

There are two basic elements in the profitability of the general, or 'composite' insurance companies (the 'composites' are the general insurance companies which undertake life assurance as well). The first is the way in which the company's premium income covers, or fails to cover, the claims and expenses on policies. The second is how the company's resources (including the premium income) generate an investment return.

The broad aim of 'underwriting' (that is, the taking of risks for an agreed sum) is to emerge breaking even over a reasonable time period. Putting the cash premiums to work creates the growth in the company's assets and income.

Insuring risks is a very competitive business and particularly so in North America. The classic pattern of competition goes like this: first, existing companies make profits on underwriting; fringe insurers are attracted into the game; they force premiums down, or keep them lower than they should be; the balance is wrong, and underwriting losses are made; the fringe operators go bust or get out; premiums can be raised; underwriting turns profitable again. Such a cycle has been repeated many times, and has usually lasted five or six years from peak to peak.

The shares of the composite insurance companies have in the past tended to fluctuate with this cycle. They have done best in the period from the low to just before the high point, and then reversed course over the next phase.

All this was complicated by the advent of high inflation. Underwriting became more difficult. The periods of loss have been rather longer and the last peak period hardly brought profit at all. Investment income has been healthy, partly because of high interest rates. The attraction of this income, perhaps, kept more fringe insurers in the game, despite the underwriting results. Thus the cycle may be lengthening.

Because of the need to maintain the fullest strength in their reserves (very important to this industry above all) the companies have periodically made heavy demands on their shareholders for new capital. This, plus the uncertainty over the underwriting cycle, kept the shares relatively depressed in the period of high inflation, outstandingly so the shares of Commercial Union (CU). But since then, the cycle *has* shown signs of an upturn and the shares have responded. At some point the market will anticipate another downturn, however!

Life insurance

Life insurance (or 'assurance' as the companies call it) is quite a different business. It is not subject to the same uncertainties as insurance against fire, flood, motor accidents and so on. Life expectancies, in aggregate, can be calculated fairly accurately. Thus all forms of simple life insurance have a stable set of premium rates and the experts (called actuaries) who work out the sums can estimate liabilities to policyholders in advance.

The difference between these liabilities and the asset values of the life fund (obtained by investing the premiums received) is called the surplus. Despite all the complications of these calculations, it is enough to say that it is all worked out very conservatively and the surpluses, which are declared every year, are arrived at after every possible provision.

Thus, unlike a company's profit, a life company's surplus is entirely free of tax and no part of it needs to be put aside.

Over the years, life assurance policies have become more and more like investment contracts. First came the endowment policy, then the 'with profits' policy. Some of the life fund surpluses go to 'with profits' policyholders. Nowadays, life companies also offer 'unit-linked' policies which are directly related to fund performance.

Of the numerous companies in the life assurance field, many are 'mutual', that is they have no shareholders and all surpluses go to policyholders. This goes for the giant, Norwich Union. However, most of the quoted companies are fairly sizeable, with the Prudential in the lead. The Pru, and Legal and General, have large business in 'general' insurance as well as life. Four companies, the biggest being Pearl, specialise in 'industrial' life business – this

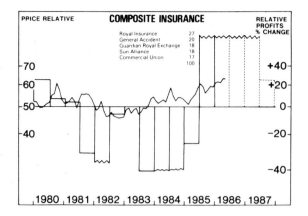

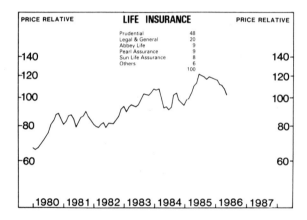

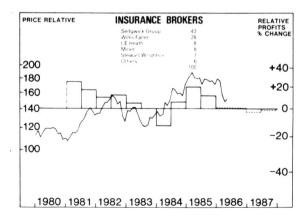

is the traditional door-to-door collection method. The two companies without any general insurance or industrial life are Equity and Law and Sun Life.

All the traditional quoted life companies, after they have declared their surpluses, allocate a proportion of this to shareholders. This proportion is on average just under 10 per cent, and it tends to remain constant; growing at the same rate as surpluses. The latter, being the result of valuations rather than variable income, have grown steadily over the years.

So the dividends from life companies can be relied upon to grow (some companies more than others) with more certainty than those from most industrial companies. For this reason, the sector traditionally had a high status (i.e. low yields) until the advent of high inflation (plus things like dividend limitation) brought poor performance in the 70s. They then staged a revival, but once more became relatively depressed when life assurance contracts lost their tax relief. They ought to be regarded as good long term investments provided that inflation does not rise substantially again.

Insurance broking companies
Insurance broking companies are not the same animals as composite or life companies, except insofar as some of them do have subsidiaries in underwriting. With most of them, the main activity is placing insurance risks with syndicates at Lloyd's, the great London centre of general insurance, and with insurance companies. They act as brokers, agents, managers. Commission on premiums, fees as agents and underwriting profit commission (where applicable) are their sources of income, and they also earn substantial sums by way of interest on premiums in transit. Lloyd's is undergoing many uncertainties at the moment, and the brokers have hived off their underwriting syndicate management business. Partly for this reason the shares no longer have the ratings which they used to hold. Much of the brokers' income comes from abroad, and they are therefore of most interest to investors who think that sterling is going to continue to decline over the years ahead.

13

Investment trusts offer a spread

Investment trusts, in their very earliest form, were designed as methods for getting British money into foreign ventures, mainly in America. Long ago, they passed through this stage and became more or less what we see today in the ordinary investment trust: a convenient method of buying a wide portfolio of shares through the medium of one. It is only very recently that some investment companies have been launched which offer something similar to those early 19th century vehicles – a stake in some risky but potentially rewarding special field, such as exploration.

There are a very large number of investment trusts (well over 200 of them are quoted in the back pages of the *Financial Times*) and they tend to come in groups under various managements. A high proportion of these management houses are stabled in Scotland because of the immense generation of private capital there during the 19th century. As a result of their international outlook, many such trusts have substantial holdings in North America. More recently, this Scottish connection helped some investment trusts to spot the possibilities of North Sea investment at an early stage.

Though the conventional investment trust holds a diversified portfolio of shares like a unit trust, and is treated for tax in largely the same way (neither investment nor authorised unit trusts, for example, pay gains tax on their own portfolio dealings), there are significant differences between the two.

Not really 'trusts', but companies
First, an investment trust is *not* a trust at all. It is a limited liability company which simply happens to be in the business of holding shares. There are certain limitations imposed by the Inland Revenue on what it must do to obtain its favoured tax treatment. These include limits on how big a percentage of its portfolio may be in any one share, and also the requirement to pay out not less than 85 per cent of its investment income. But otherwise it can behave as a company.

An investment trust can, for example, raise more capital either through an issue of its own shares, or by borrowing the money through an issue of fixed interest stock. Considerable advantages were gained by investment trusts in the era of very low interest rates by the issue of loan stocks. The growth of income and of capital was enhanced for the equity shareholders. Existing loan stocks issued in those years still provide some 'gearing', although the effect is now much less upon the current, higher, base of income. The issue of loan stocks at the sort of interest rates we have seen in recent years has not been very attractive.

Of course, gearing can work both ways. Thus a geared investment trust can look more or less attractive than an ungeared investment such as a unit trust, depending on what you think the market in which it is primarily invested is going to do.

Asset values versus market prices

The concept of investment trusts looking more or less atractive than the value of their underlying investments brings us to another important difference between investment and unit trusts. The latter are priced to reflect the valuation of these investments, more or less exactly, and usually every day. The buying and selling of units by investors does not normally disturb this valuation to any significant degree. However, investment trusts are companies with an equity capital which is fixed unless rights issues are made.

Thus the buying and selling of investment trust shares *does* affect their market price. If for any reason a trust becomes attractive enough to investors, its share price can rise above its asset value – it will stand at 'premium', likewise, if it loses attraction, the shares can fall below the asset value and will stand at a 'discount'.

For a long time now, for most investment trusts, discounts have been the rule. The chart shows the average discount in recent years. Investment trust shares in the decade to 1980 by and large lost popularity, causing a trend towards an increasing discount. The actual portfolio performance was not on the whole too bad, but the share performance was disappointing.

This trend seems to have reversed since 1980 though as in the past the fluctuations are considerable. Currently, the average discount on asset values is 25 per cent. Most trusts are on discounts quite close to this, though in a minority of cases the discount is substantially more and a few trusts, at the other end of the scale of attraction, actually stand at a premium to assets.

These figures are abstracted from one of the detailed computerised estimates, produced daily by many leading stockbroking firms for all trusts. As second best, the Association of Investment Trust Companies itself publishes a table every fourth Saturday of the month in the *Financial Times* and the *Daily Telegraph*, giving asset values and five-year performance records amongst other material.

As you would expect, the portfolio performance of different trusts has varied from poor to excellent over the years, and this is usually reflected in the size of the discount. But history is not the full explanation of discounts. The trusts which are on the biggest premiums may often be those where expectations of future performance have most influence.

Turning away from these speculative high flyers, however, what chance is there that middle of the road trusts with reasonable portfolio records, on average discounts, will do well in future? If interest rates show clear signs of coming down decisively, trust discounts will probably contract, giving extra share performance.

But one other factor is worth remembering. The narrowing of discounts since 1980 which we have noted was caused in part by a number of bids for investment trusts, or by moves to turn certain investment trusts into unit

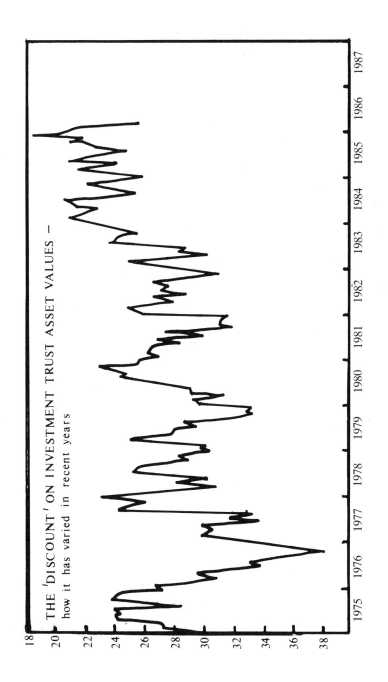

THE 'DISCOUNT' ON INVESTMENT TRUST ASSET VALUES –
how it has varied in recent years

trusts. Insurance companies and pension funds may be tempted to take over an investment trust as a way of getting their hands on a high quality portfolio of investments at one swoop.

Either a bid or 'unitisation' is likely to mean that the shareholder in the investment trust receives, in one form or another, something near full asset value for his shares. A number of investors are prepared to tuck away investment trust shares on the assumption they will benefit in this way from elimination of the discount at some stage in the future.

Split capital investment trusts

A specialised variant on the investment trust theme is the 'split capital' investment trust. There are over a score of these special trusts. Each has two forms of capital. With one, the shares get all the income from the underlying investments, but are only repaid at par value, or some other specified amount, on a set liquidation date. With the other form of capital, shareholders get no income but have the right to all the assets, on the set liquidation date, over and above the sum repayable to the income shareholders.

These trusts offer clear advantage to investors at either end of the income scale. Their liquidation dates vary, so there are many investment permutations. For those strictly interested in capital performance, the capital shares of trusts with, say, ten to fifteen years to go, have large discounts on their underlying asset values. These should be realisable as an ultimate 'backstop', whilst earlier performance is probable if the stockmarket does well. Income seekers should go for longer dated trusts with a good record of dividend increases. Shares with this background can not be treated as 'fixed income' stocks. They can offer an initial high yield with a rising stream of income, which could well suit a low taxpayer (such as a retired person on a modest pension). The disadvantage is that their ultimate liquidation prices are often lower than the current market values. But the likely 'total return' for the sort of holder I mentioned above may be very attractive. You should of course consult your stockbroker about the suitability of either capital or the income options of these trusts.

14

How to evaluate property companies

Property plays a particularly important part in British commercial life, both as an investment in its own right and as a security for various forms of lending. For the individual investor, shares in a quoted property company are usually the most attractive way of sharing in the growth of commercial property values.

The traditional property investment company has a number of characteristics that separate it from manufacturing or service concerns. Usually it shows a relatively low current yield and the shares are bought mainly for long-term capital and income growth. The company may finance itself to a greater extent on borrowed money than most manufacturing concerns could or would care to do, and it is likely to pay out a higher proportion of its earnings by way of dividend.

The importance of asset backing

Though the property company's shares will be valued partly according to their yield, the asset backing is at least as important a factor. If all the liabilities of the company are deducted from the value of the properties and any other assets it owns, the resultant sum is what belongs to the shareholders. Divided by the number of shares, this gives a figure for the 'net asset value per share'. The market value of the shares will normally stand somewhat below this. You will often see shares in a property company described as giving such-and-such a yield and 'standing at a discount of (say) 25 per cent to net assets'.

This does not mean that the company necessarily has any intention of selling its properties, or that the shareholder would necessarily receive as much as net asset value for his shares if it did – capital gains tax on disposal of the properties might have to be paid. It is more of a yardstick for comparing one company with another, and can also serve as an indicator of income growth in the future. The relationship between share price and net asset value can, of course, fluctuate within quite wide limits.

Residential property now unpopular

The majority of quoted property companies today invest mainly in commercial and industrial property: in other words, in office buildings, shops, warehouses and factories. Residential property has become increasingly unpopular as an income-yielding investment because of rent controls and other restrictions imposed by successive governments.

Most property companies will have a fair mix of different kinds of commercial property though some will tend to specialise in one type: shops (as the name applies) in the case of London Shop Property Trust, or factory and warehouse buildings in the case of Slough Estates. Companies may also specialise by geographical area. The biggest of them all, the Land Securities Investment Trust, has a spread of different types of top quality commercial and industrial property throughout the United Kingdom, but is probably best known for its portfolio of office properties in Central London.

Other companies hold a fair proportion of their properties overseas, particularly in Australia and in Continental Europe, with the occasional incursion into North America. Not all of these overseas ventures have met with total success.

Property companies differ not only by geographical location and by the type of property they own. The nature of the operation they undertake will also differ. The commercial property investment company of which we have spoken so far does much of what its name suggests: it owns properties and (hopefully) sees its income and the value of its assets rise as inflation and shortage force rents upwards. Many are now reaping the rewards from properties constructed twenty years ago. If the income comes entirely from rents from well-located properties, this income is of very high quality. Up to a point its growth can be predicted. Even on the basis of today's rental levels it may be clear that a building will show an increase in income when the lease comes up for review.

Heyday of property development

In practice, many property *investment* companies started out as property *development* companies (a higher risk, higher reward business) and some still undertake developments as well. In the development boom days of the 1950s and early 1960s the name of the game was to raise long-term finance in the form of a mortgage of two-thirds of the value of a completed development at a fixed rate of interest from (then less inflation-conscious) insurance companies. Provided the development was valued at 50 per cent or more above what it cost, they recouped the whole of the outlay and the surplus belonged to the shareholders, as did any subsequent rise in the value of the building. Many property companies have cheap borrowings dating back to those days. But nowadays rates for fixed interest money are too high; inflation-conscious insurance companies want a share in any growth from the building; and current developments are more likely to be financed by some form of partnership arrangement between property company and financial institution.

Other property companies develop buildings to sell at a capital profit on completion rather than to retain for their rents, and still others make a trade of buying and selling properties without undertaking development. Profit from these sources is not as stable – or, therefore, as valuable – as income from rents, though it can sometimes be a useful addition. Hence rule number one: see where a property company's income comes from and of what 'quality' it is. This can vary dramatically.

Rule number two for property company investors is to take expert advice: this is a specialist sector of the market in which a very few firms of stockbrokers have a particular expertise.

Third, comes a note of caution. Bricks and mortar are a sound investment, but not in any condition at any price. The virtue of commercial properties is that the financial institutions invest directly in them on a large scale, so there are usually ready buyers for a property company's assets.

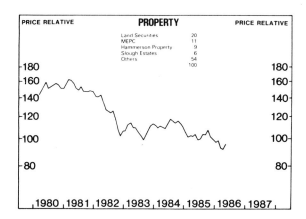

But not always. The market in investment properties almost dried up in the financial crash of 1974-75 and values slumped drastically. Property companies which had undertaken too many developments on the back of borrowed short-term money found themselves unable to borrow more to pay the interest and unable to sell the properties to repay the debt. A number went bust, others had to cut drastically. It is less likely to happen today. But remember that a property development eats up cash rather than producing it, until it is completed and has found a tenant. A massive development programme can be a mixed blessing.

Over the early eighties, most property shares were relatively indifferent investments. Comparatively few modern developments took place. There now appears to be a revival under way, but there is still a shortage. Companies with good existing properties and/or good developments ought to benefit from this, provided that inflation does not continue to decline.

15

Understanding the oil market

Oil companies have been right in the middle of the two most important economic phenomena in Britain's post-war history. The first, shared by the rest of the world, was the 1973 oil crisis and its successor in 1979. The second was, of course, the almost simultaneous rise of North Sea oil production.

The oil price boom
The oil crisis was precipitated in 1973 by the Arab/Israeli war and the oil embargo. How the Western world laid itself open to this crisis is another story, highly disputed. Suffice it to say that, whereas in early 1973 the price of crude oil, at around $2 per barrel (about 35 gallons) was not much different from what it had been half a century before, by the end of 1973 it had suddenly become $11.

A fivefold increase in basic product price is quite a transformation, for existing companies, for aspiring companies, and for the consumer. As might be expected, many of the international oil 'majors' made massive stock profits. However, they finally lost control of their Middle Eastern production. The governments in that area took over official sales of oil. This greatly limited the companies' flexibility in dealing with the product. Moreover, although the companies made stock profits, they had to face a dramatic fall in demand, then a world financial crisis, involving their tanker fleet amongst other factors.

There followed three relatively calm years for the oil price. It rose modestly but did not keep up with general inflation. Profits of the big 'internationals' behaved in much the same way, though they were on a higher plateau than before 1973. Then in 1979 came the Iranian revolution, followed later by the Iranian/Iraqi war. Over the course of 1979, the free market oil price trebled, from $13 to $38 per barrel. Thus over six years the crude oil price had risen twentyfold.

From that peak, oil prices declined, but remained above the $30 level until 1986, when, with a suddenness equal to that of 1973, they dropped to below $10 at one point. At what price they will find a stable level remains to be seen.

The rise of North Sea Oil
Meanwhile, UK North Sea oil production rose steeply, from almost zero in 1975 to 2.5 billion barrels per day in 1986. Within this period Britain entered the top ten of oil-producing countries.

This is the background to the oil shares market in the UK. It explains why the shares of UK based oil companies rose substantially more than average over the period from 1974 to late 1980. It also explains why they fell during the years that followed. Naturally, the shares of the initially tiny North Sea exploration companies performed, in varying degrees, very much better than those of the existing widely spread big companies. By the same token, they have been and still are more 'volatile'. The chart does not show the good 1974 to 1980 performance, only the decline since then, with the beginnings of a recovery. But you may note that the 'relative' number of 320 at the peak is a measure of how good the sector has been, and could be again if another oil famine develops.

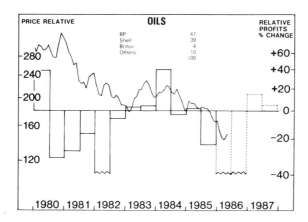

The most volatile stage of all is that of exploration. In the case of the small company which is mainly dedicated to exploration, this reflects fully in the share-price, of course. The heyday of exploration in the North Sea is now long over, but there are still some specialist companies exploring in the USA, where the official price of oil has been freed from Government control. There are also some in the UK seeking oil and gas on land. The values of such companies' shares, if they are mainly explorers, depend primarily on whether they find oil at all. If and when a discovery is made, the value of the shares then depends on the significance of the find to the company – its size relative to the other interests – and the likely price of the oil when sold.

Then comes the preparation for production. This is where more money has to be raised, to cover costs which in the North Sea are a heavy initial item (but are not so onerous in Dorset farmland!). To cover exploration and pre-production costs, many complicated methods of finance have been used in recent years by the smaller companies. A discovery may be sold off, in whole or part, to another party better equipped to raise money on its own. Thus an exploration company may continue to specialise, financing itself by sales of discoveries.

At the pre-production stage, more is known about the 'field' and the return on the capital involved is roughly calculable by the company (if not always by the outside shareholders). The company's risks are less. Thus at this stage the share price is often showing its maximum return to the speculative shareholder, and he may sell, causing a dip in the price.

The more advanced phases of production are normally less exciting, but the returns available are still highly geared to the price of oil. Thus, in the North Sea, where the 1979 oil crisis occurred as many production projects were beginning to accelerate, the shares in this category gained a new lease of life. A case in point was LASMO, which was formed in 1971, and eventually acquired a large minority interest (alongside BP) in the giant 'Ninian' field, discovered in 1974. Production began in late 1978 and the shares had been drifting downwards. Then came the problems in Iran, and LASMO shares rose from 150p to a peak of 875p in late 1980. As the price of oil fell in 1981/82, LASMO shares also fell, but rather more steeply. You can see from the chart of LASMO's 1986 decline that this high oil price gearing works in reverse as well.

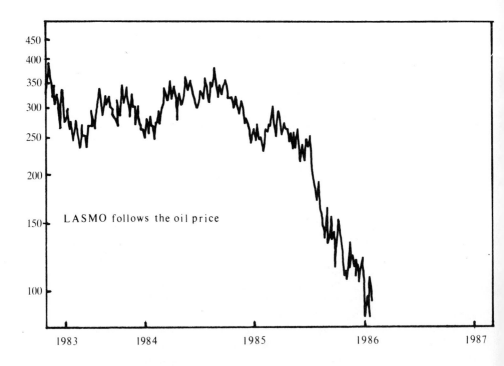

LASMO follows the oil price

The next stages in the development of an integrated oil company are those of refining and distribution (known as 'downstream activities'). This is where the high risk/reward nature of oil exploration gives way to a more conventional industrial character. The international 'majors' such as BP and Shell Transport (the UK partner in the Royal Dutch/Shell group) have large interests in these activities, which were set up to give the oil companies more control over the markets in their products. From time to time these activities may carry disadvantages. For some time after 1980 reduced demand for petroleum products in Europe hit BP and Shell refinery and distribution profits very hard, but the fall in oil prices over 1986 did much to restore these.

In any case, a widely diversified international oil group is not going to be as profitable as a successful exploration or pure production company. But note the word 'successful'; if an exploration company finds nothing it could end up worth nothing.

What the shares of the oil majors offer is the prospect of relatively consistent growth in earnings. During periods of uncertainty in demand, the ratings of the shares will tend to be low. But when stability returns to the oil market, growth should be resumed.

16

Thrills and spills in mining shares

Mining, for an investor, involves somewhat similar concepts to those discussed in the chapter on oil. The process of mining involves exploration, discovery, appraisal and production. The degree of risk, and potential reward, lessens as you come up the scale. Finance is needed for exploration as with oil. But the financing of production is usually much more expensive than with oil, profitability is not so intrinsically high, and therefore taxation by host governments is not so great either.

Metal prices fluctuate in cycles

There are important differences, however, in the mature stages of production of metals and oil. Unlike the oil price before 1973, the consumer prices of metals have always fluctuated widely with the cycles in world demand, and thus mining operators have traditionally been 'speculative' in this respect. Since the beginning of the 1970s, with its huge rise in inflation and then the subsequent fall, the metal price fluctuations have been wider. Thus, whilst many mining shares have outperformed UK share market averages, this has included periods of relative boom and slump in the shares.

There are of course many different metals, and though there are very rough correspondences between their price cycles, such as obtained in periods of peak industrial demand or in a recessionary trough, they are by no means close enough to affect metals identically, nor the shares most closely associated with each.

Base metals and precious metals

Commercially there are two main categories of metal, first, 'base' metals such as copper, lead and zinc, and, second, the precious metals, gold, silver and platinum. Prices are the obvious difference, but for investment purposes, the distinction is more fundamentally between those which are mainly affected by industrial demand, and those which are also seen as inflation 'hedges' or investments in their own right.

For most ordinary investors the really important distinction is between gold and the rest. This is because gold has been, throughout history, the chief measure of monetary value in the long term, even if there is now no official link with currencies. So the course of the gold price will continue to be linked mainly to hopes and fears about world inflation, through the medium of the principal currency of influence, the US dollar.

THE GOLD PRICE IN RECENT YEARS (in US$)

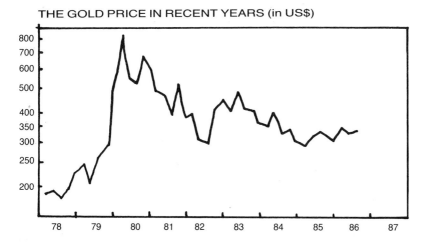

There are many relatively small mining companies, mainly in the US and Australia, which specialise in mining exploration, and others which concentrate on one metal. But for the small investor in the UK the most convenient investments are the big mining groups which have diversified their interests.

The groups which are registered in Australia, South Africa and North America, though foreign, are nowadays well known in the UK. However the UK registered 'mining finance houses' cover a big enough field to start with. Of these, Charter Consolidated is now comparatively little involved in mining. Consolidated Goldfields, however, is very substantially interested in gold mining through its subsidiary company in South Africa. The third, Rio Tinto Zinc (RTZ) has wide interests throughout the world, direct and indirect, in many 'base' minerals.

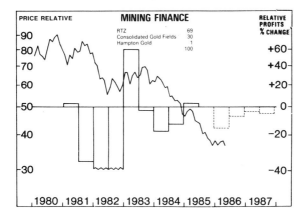

The tradition of interlinked holdings, and joint investment in different projects, is strong within the sector. It arises from the need to spread risk and lighten the financial burdens of development.

The share ratings of the big mining groups naturally reflect this relative stability, yields being lower than they would otherwise be if there were no such stabilising influence. However, ratings vary widely nonetheless, according to the weightings of different groups' 'portfolios' of minerals, and on the investment view of the prospects in each. Worldwide, Australian mining house shares have tended to have the highest ratings, because of the relative political certainty and the assurance of investment funds for promising projects. The lowest current ratings tend to be in those with a high proportion of South African gold mining interests.

The South African gold scene is best reflected in the shares of the individual gold mines themselves. These are the 'raw material' from which the various finance houses draw their income, and in which they play a management role. There are currently 40 mines, separately quoted in Johannesburg and London. There are active deals in most of them, many City institutions being involved. Over the years since the great Rand discoveries, the industry has settled into a well-defined structure. The mines vary in size; in the grades of production and of reserves (i.e. the quality of the ore); and in the estimated 'lives' of the mines (the latter vary from under ten to twenty years). They also vary in their costs of extraction of ore, according to the depths or difficulties of the 'reef'.

Though a number of these factors can be estimated quite accurately, in the world as we now know it there is no guarantee on either costs or prices. Thus the shares are highly volatile. There are also fluctuations in currency exchange rates. Added to which, of course, is the intangible South African political uncertainty,which, as we have recently seen, becomes of paramount importance at certain times.

F.T. GOLD MINES INDEX

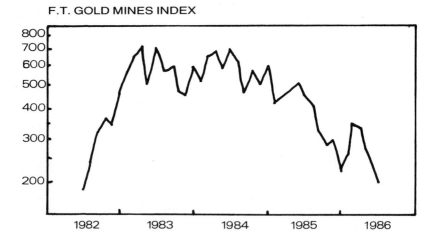

Because of the high 'gearing' of operational results to the gold price, the earnings of the mines (and therefore their dividends because most of their profits are distributed) have risen and fallen dramatically. Partly because of this intrinsic uncertainty, and partly because of the political dimension, the actual returns to the investor have been handsome over the years in terms of dividend yields.

For those whose chief aim is capital appreciation, investment in the mines is a much trickier business: very profitable if one guesses it right and *vice versa!* A lot of background knowledge is necessary, and so is a close watch on the market. Most people will prefer the indirect route, through a mining finance house, or through a unit trust specialising in this area.

More speculative still, of course, are the pure exploration companies which proliferate particularly in Australia, and where a 'find' or rumours of a find can bring dramatic share price movements. This is an area where local knowledge counts for a great deal, and UK investors should be aware of the often very high risks. The dramatic rise and subsequent fall of Poseidon in the previous Australian exploration boom was one example. There have been more recent ones in the period since 1982.

17

Overseas trading companies
A hedge against sterling and the UK economy

Most of the profits of the companies which are now loosely called 'overseas traders' are indeed earned overseas. The name has been more widely used since the Financial Times Actuaries created a new sub-index with this title in 1975, but it has a long-standing connotation in the stockmarket. It refers more to their ultimate origins than to their current mixture of business.

They are in fact the inheritors of the original ventures that took the British to far corners of the globe and laid the background for its erstwhile dominance of world trade. The old East India Company has long gone, and the 'big picture' has changed. But along with other strands in the network (such as the much reduced shipping interests, and the still active overseas banking in the Far East and Africa) the talents and the know-how which the British deployed in trade are still at work in many companies.

A basis in commodities
The common factors between these companies are their strong links with local interests in the traditional British spheres of influence overseas, and a basis in the production, processing and/or trading in commodities. These include rubber, palm oil, tea, coffee, cocoa and sugar. Some are involved in the meat trade including livestock. Some are in timber. Most of them have developed or acquired other interests and these include transport, distribution and manufacturing, but again with a common thread of local overseas participation. Where they have developed in the UK this has usually been for strictly 'defensive' reasons, to support their overseas efforts, or for tax purposes. The latter is a consequence of the need to pay dividends to their UK shareholders, which are always taxed, but where this tax can be offset against actual taxable profits in Britian.

Rubber and palm oil
The most important commodity represented is rubber, along with its associate crop, palm oil. Most of the world's natural rubber still comes from Malaysia: the system of plantations on which rubber growing is based is a British creation, as is the more recent development of palm oil. You will still find rubber plantation shares in the *Financial Times* back pages under that heading. Most of these are now registered in Malaysia, since the policy of the

Malaysian government is to achieve local shareholding, and ultimate control in some cases, over a planned time period. The British-owned plantation management groups have gradually ceded more and more to local interests.

Sime Darby and Guthrie are now Malaysian controlled. But the biggest single rubber group, Harrisons and Crosfield, is still very much British owned, still runs plantations, and still holds a shareholding in a Malaysian plantation company, (though this company, Harrisons Malaysian Estates, is now controlled in Malaysia).

The shares of this group, and other rubber-oriented UK companies, have in the recent past been boosted by the speculation of Malaysian acquisition of the UK shares. This ferment is now over. But the underlying attraction of rubber and palm oil, harvested ever more efficiently, remains even though these commodities have shared the decline in prices seen during 1985 and 1986.

Indeed, despite the wide geographical spread in this sector, the growth and prosperity of South East Asia has been one of the strong themes in the activities of the companies concerned. Inchcape, with interests in tea and timber amongst other commodities, made its biggest profits in recent years out of the distribution of Toyota motor vehicles in this area.

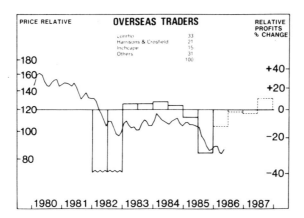

Of course, there are a number of 'ex-colonial' trading companies based in Hong Kong and therefore (unlike the ones we are talking about) technically foreign despite their British ownership and management. The UK trading companies and those in Hong Kong have joint interests in some cases. One of the important factors in operations from the 'entrepot' centres of the Far East is that (despite the 'China Question' in Hong Kong) there is no trend towards state appropriation of expatriate enterprises.

This has been the bugbear of those companies operating in Africa other than South Africa. Companies like Mitchell Cotts, once big owners and managers of cotton, tea, grain and other agricultural estates in Northern and East Africa, have virtually migrated south, to the Republic, developing into industrial services and into manufacturing proper. Paterson Zochonis, on the other hand, has learnt to live with the difficulties of Nigeria, its biggest single area of activity.

Some of the companies have expanded by acquisition in a very big way. The prime example is Dalgety, which from its original pastoral actvities in

Australia and New Zealand has extended its agricultural and food interests, and now, embracing Spillers, is more than half in the UK.

It is indeed quite common for companies which make acquisitions into anything other than closely related fields to run into difficulties. Some overseas traders who have bought UK businesses (because of the dividend taxation problem referred to earlier) have found it hardly worthwhile. Inchcape found this with Mann Egerton, the BL motor distributors.

Clearly, one of the important characteristics of the overseas traders is their independence of sterling. This offers advantages if sterling is going to resume its post-war trend towards depreciation, interrupted as this was in 1979 and 1980 by the combination of the oil price and the North Sea. Another characteristic, shared in greater or lesser degree, is the ability to participate in faster-growing areas of the world. The disadvantages include the cyclical nature of commodity prices (though this is lessened by diversification in the commodities) and in some cases, political risks. The chart shows how the sector has been hit by the commodity cycle in the 1985-86 period. Nevertheless, the leading companies in the sector offer an important element of choice to the UK investor.

18

Investing abroad: high risks for high rewards

In an 'open economy' like the UK, overseas influences are considerable. International trends in interest rates and commodity prices are passed on to UK markets directly or indirectly. The exports of British companies are affected by overseas conditions. Moreover, many British companies (particularly those companies whose shares are quoted on the Stock Exchange) have activities abroad. Indeed, there are substantial direct investments and certain sectors, such as mining, overseas trading and oil, where you will find companies with very little UK activity at all. Thus, there is a large element of choice in overseas investment 'exposure' within UK registered companies.

However, this is not quite the same as participation in overseas share markets, which are directly related to their own domestic economies and financial conditions.

Markets and currencies may vary widely
Motives for investing abroad may include a desire for 'diversification' in this respect. Because other areas of the world are not doing the same thing at the same time, their share markets may also be performing differently. The currencies of the countries involved, as compared with sterling, may be changing also, either accentuating or diminishing the effect of the local market change.

But every investor hopes to get something more than just diversification, and the point of overseas investment for an individual must be to get into more profitable or faster-growing areas than UK investment can give directly.

This, by definition, involves more risk. The first hurdle is in choosing which particular overseas area or areas, and the second hurdle is in the timing of your dealings. These are really two faces of the same problem. The third hurdle is stock selection.

To take the last point first: there are *some* short cuts, in the shape of well known shares, many of which are actually *quoted* on the London Stock Exchange. Examples are IBM, Ford Motor, Exxon Corporation. Most are American-based but by virtue of their size and spread they can be viewed very much against an international background. Others, like Hongkong & Shanghai Bank, are familiar investments to most UK stockbrokers (and in this case represent a fair sized slice of the whole Hong Kong economy!).

U.K. (FTA ALL SHARE INDEX)

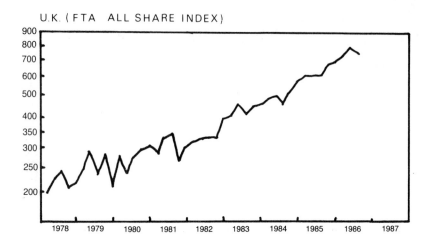

U.S. MARKET (STANDARD & POOR'S INDEX)

GERMAN MARKET (COMMERZBANK INDEX)

There has always been a lot of local knowledge of major Australian and South African mining stocks. Some London brokers also cover the major industrial and commercial investments in those areas.

I will not go into the methods and costs of dealing, except to say that London *dealing* will involve the usual commission and so on, and that foreign dealing can be cheaper but is a lot more bother unless your London broker has an overseas office. You should be able to get specific advice from your stockbroker on the best policy to pursue.

JAPANESE INDEX

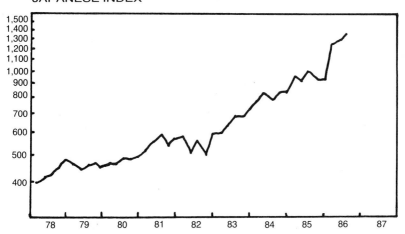

HONG KONG INDEX

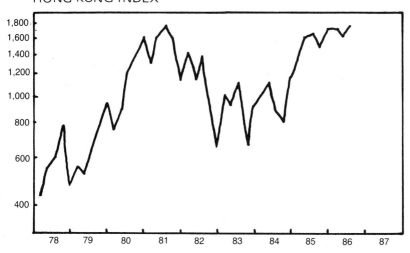

If you want to switch easily into or out of your chosen areas, without incurring the additional problem of share selection, there are of course many investment trusts and unit trusts which specialise in one or other overseas market, and which offer the spread you need. You still have the risks attached to these markets, and their fluctuations.

No problem now with the 'dollar premium'

There is one risk you no longer have to run, however. Until 1979, overseas portfolio investment was only possible through the medium of 'investment currency'. This was a pool of dollars, limited in size, into which you had to buy in order then to exchange these dollars for your actual currency of choice. Investment currency itself had a price, a 'premium' on the dollar, which fluctuated, sometimes dramatically.

It made the choice of final investment secondary to the risks of the 'premium'. This grotesque set-up has now been dismantled but I mention it because there is no guarantee that something like it will not be introduced again. At that stage, if it occurs, the advantage may be to the investor already into the foreign currency.

Setting this speculation aside, however, there is still likely to be a lot of difference in market fluctuations between the UK and elsewhere, and between sterling and different currencies.

There has always been an international winner in any one short period, say twelve months or so, but this has seldom been followed up by another similar performance in subsequent periods. Thus the timing of investment overseas has been particularly crucial, reflecting as it does both market and currency moves. It has often been right to follow the old investment rule, so difficult to put into practice, of selling when enthusiasm for a particular market or currency has become general.

Despite these evident disadvantages, there still remains the equally evident fact, displayed over many years, of higher growth in many overseas economies than in the UK. This is not evident in the USA in general, but it is in the Californian and South Western states, where many investment funds have concentrated in recent years. Nor was it the case in Europe for many years, until the bull markets of 1984-86 put the rest of the world into the shade.

High growth in the Far East – but wide fluctuations

It has been the case in Japan and Far Eastern markets, where there are also quite a number of investment funds to choose from. These markets have been based on economic and financial trends markedly different from those in the West. In this respect they have certainly been a 'hedge'. Their fluctuations have been sometimes almost the converse of those in the UK. In Hong Kong and Singapore, the degree of fluctuation has been occasionally hair-raising. But overall, their growth has been very much greater. The Japanese market, as befits the best-organised economy in the world, has not seen wild fluctuations. The currency has made up for this, showing great strength most of the time, alarming weakness occasionally, significant overall appreciation.

There are some tax disadvantages in overseas investment where income is involved. Investment funds will pay a higher total rate of tax than on UK income, and this will not always be reclaimable by a UK holder of such funds. Nevertheless, in the higher growth areas, income yield will nearly always be a relatively small part of the total investment return.

19

What scrip issues are all about

Having covered some of the main sectors of the market, I want now to return to the investment arithmetic to explain in more detail some of the phenomena with which any shareholder needs to familiarise himself.

Let us start with the 'scrip' or 'capitalisation' issue of shares. The first that you as a shareholder in a company will probably know about it is when you read in the press or hear from the company direct that it is planning to make such an issue. Stripped of the financial jargon, the statement will say that, subject to shareholders' approval, all shareholders will be receiving additional new shares in such-and-such a proportion to those they already hold.

Scrip issues don't give you anything for nothing

The shareholder is not required to put up any extra money, which is why a scrip issue is often loosely referred to as a 'free' or 'bonus' issue. But in practice there is no such thing as a free lunch, and the shareholder is not getting anything for nothing.

In fact, a scrip issue is really just a book-keeping transaction, but since it leads to an adjustment in the price of the shares, it is important to see how and why it arises. When a company starts from scratch its issued capital usually compares closely with its assets. Over the years these assets grow as profits are ploughed back and values rise. But the issued ordinary capital stays at the same nominal amount until it is specifically changed by further issues. In terms of the company's balance sheet, the net assets of a company are reflected in the capital plus the reserves. With the capital fixed, the growth of the net assets is directly reflected in the 'reserves' figure.

To take an extreme example, where no further ordinary capital had been issued, we might get after many years a company with an issued ordinary capital of £100,000 in £1 shares, but whose net assets were £10m. This would be defined in the balance sheet at £100,000 capital plus £9.9m of reserves.

This company could be earning, say, £1m before tax on the assets, a return of only 10 per cent. But in terms of its tiny equity capital the earnings and dividends would seem immense. You can do the sums: assuming corporation tax at about 50 per cent, the company's net earnings (if there are no prior charges) would be £500,000, or five times the nominal ordinary capital. So earnings per share would be £5, and dividends, if half the earnings were distributed, would be £2.50 per share. Another peculiarity about this company would be the share price. If the shares were valued in the stockmarket at, say, a PE ratio of 10 (ten times earnings) they would be £50 each. If, for any special reasons, they were regarded as being worth their net asset value, they would stand at £100 each.

Before the scrip issue	After a scrip issue of
Issued Ordinary capital	ninety-nine to one
(in 100,000 £1 shares)................................ £100,000	£10,000,000
Reserves..£9,900,000	Nil
Capital and Reserves £10,000,000	£10,000,000
Net assets per share £100	100p

Now, suppose the directors, reckoning that the price of the individual shares was too unwieldy and that the issued share capital in no way reflected the capital really used in the business, decided to make a scrip issue of 99 new ordinary shares for every one already held. This would be a 'capitalisation' of the £9.9m reserves, turning them – together with the existing £100,000 of shares – into a new enlarged ordinary capital of £10m. The arithmetic per share would change dramatically, though if all else is equal the value of your holding would not change. After the issue you would have 100 shares for every one before, but the 100 would be worth the same amount in aggregate as the single share was before. Earnings per share would be 5p, dividends per share (if strictly scaled down) would be 2.5p and if the shares were rated on a PE of 10, the market price would be 50p, or if they were rated at net asset value the price would be 100p.

However, the normal sort of scrip issue is not, of course, of those proportions. Most companies like to keep up with the growth in their assets or 'reserves' to express them in their balance sheet context before this level of disparity is reached.

Thus, a typical scrip issue could be a 'one-for-one' (a 100 per cent capitalisation), a 'one-for-two' (a 50 per cent capitalisation), a 'one-for-three' (a 33.3 per cent) and so on.

Don't lose touch with scrip issues

A one-for-one scrip issue is easiest to deal with in your own accounting. Every figure which is in 'per share' terms will be halved after a one-for-one scrip: earnings per share, dividend per share, asset value per share, and market value of the share. But you will have to be more watchful for the effects of smaller proportionate scrip issues, particularly if they are a regular feature of company policy. Many a shareholder has lost track of his real progress by forgetting to adjust for minor scrip issues in the past.

Suppose you had purchased your shares at 25p and the scrip issue is in the ratio of one new share for every four held. You will end up with five shares where you had four before, so your 'effective' purchase price is adjusted down to 20p (25p × 4/5).

This will give you the necessary reference point needed to chart your holding in future years. Do this for every scrip issue: in other words, adjust your previously adjusted figure in the same way, cumulatively altering it for each subsequent scrip issue.

HOW SCRIP ISSUES CAN ADD UP: KEEP ADJUSTING!

Terms of scrip issue	Adjustment factor	Purchase price per share	Number of shares
		25p	1,000
one for four	× 4/5	20p	1,250
one for three	× 3/4	15p	1,666
one for five	× 5/6	12.5p	2,000

The timetable of a scrip issue is roughly as follows: the company's directors propose the issue and an increase in the company's authorised share capital if necessary. This proposal is passed at a meeting, for which you have a vote. The company issues 'allotment letters' which you will normally accept. The original shares go 'ex scrip' (this is when the market price of the old shares is adjusted downwards by the appropriate fraction), and are first quoted as old shares and new shares separately. Then finally both forms of share resume a unified quotation.

You will, of course, normally accept the new shares. If you wish to sell them, in their initial form as allotment letters, you may do so but you will be diminishing your investment in the company.

The shares are usually quoted 'ex-cap' (in fact they will be marked 'ex c.' in newspaper quotations) on the first business day after the letters are posted. Before this, anyone buying the shares is buying them with the right to the new shares ('cum cap'). After they go ex-cap, he will be only buying either old or new shares, at the adjusted price.

20

When a company makes a rights issue – the shareholder's sums

Rights issues are a very different matter from scrip issues. The company in this case is asking its shareholders for cash. You, as a shareholder, are faced with the choice of providing this, or not. But the mechanics of a rights issue do not allow you to ignore the implications for your existing holding.

Rights issues were evolved as the fairest practical method a company can employ to raise more equity capital. It is not, of course, the only way companies raise more cash: they may well raise money through borrowings of various kinds; indeed, this is a continuing process with most of them. Borrowings are a matter of shareholder interest, too, insofar as the degree of borrowing may be excessive, or the cost of it too steep. But assuming that the company's directors know their business, this borrowing ought to produce a surplus return for the shareholders and its cost is fixed, at any rate in terms of the outgoing interest rate.

New equity capital, however, has no fixed cost. It takes a share in earnings and dividends, in perpetuity, from existing shareholders. The principle has therefore been established that equity issues are normally offered to existing shareholders first, in proportion to their holdings. Another, less fair, type of issue has been gaining ground in recent times, known as the 'vendor placing', which I will refer to later.

Reactions to an issue

The most important underlying factors in any rights issues are the factors which always concern shareholders: how profitable is the company, what are its immediate trading prospects, how are its finances progressing? These will condition the stock market's reaction to the call for new cash, and the amount which the company wants to raise will also be part and parcel of this reaction. If the company is very profitable and is doing very well, the issue may be greeted in a buoyant fashion. If the reserve is the case, it may not be popular. We shall look at some of these permutations in a later context. However, whatever the background, the mechanics of a rights issue allow the company to go ahead in all but the most extreme of bearish market conditions by varying the terms of its issue.

Suppose a company with an issued equity capital of 1,000,000 shares of 25p nominal value, standing at 200p in the market, wants to raise £375,000. This is a substantial issue in relation to the company's existing value in the market (200p × 1m = £2m). There may well be a fear that the market price will weaken. Thus, the company will not want to offer the new shares at anywhere near 200p, or it might not get any subscribers. So it must offer them at a reasonable 'discount'. It may decide to make an issue of one new share for every four held, at a price of 150p. This would cope with most of the risks of market fluctuation. However, if the directors were very cautious they could just as well offer one new share for every two held, at a price of 75p. This would raise exactly the same amount. The discount to the market price is greater but the number of shares created is also greater.

SHARE PRICES AS A FUNCTION OF ISSUE TERMS
(Company share capital 1,000,000, market price 200p each)
1. Issue 187,500 shares at 200p = £375,000
2. Issue 250,000 shares at 150p = £375,000
3. Issue 500,000 shares at 75p = £375,000

You must always bear in mind that whatever this discount, you are not being offered something for nothing. The value of your total holding will not be changed, except by the cash that you put up (and, one must add, except for any changes in the 'rating' of the shares which might follow from the reaction to the issue).

Consider the arithmetic of the one-for-four issue at 150p. Your existing holding is, say, four shares at 200p each. If you subscribe to the issue, you will pay 150p and receive one more share. The value of your five shares will then be no more than the sum of all these, thus: $(4 \times 200p) + (1 \times 150p) = 800p + 150p = 950p$ or 190p for each of the five shares you end up with.

This figure of 190p is in fact the theoretical 'ex rights' price of the shares after the issue (theoretical because the market can always force this up or down, which is a real change in value).

If the terms of the issue had been one new share for two at 75p, the arithmetic would be: 2 shares at 200p = 400p plus one new share at 75p = 475p in aggregate for three shares, or 158.3p for each share 'ex rights'. So the larger the discount, the lower will be the price of your shares after the issue, and you will see from the above how to calculate this effect. You may also realise that if your total investment value is unchanged, and yet your market share price has dropped, the operation contains some element of a scrip issue as well as of a capital-raising operation.

THREE POSSIBLE ISSUES (BUT ONE UNLIKELY!)

Market price before issue	Terms of issue	Subscription price of new shares	Calculation of ex-rights price	Theoretical ex-rights price
200p	three for sixteen	200p	$\dfrac{(16\times200p) + (3\times200p)}{19} =$	200p
200p	one for four	150p	$\dfrac{(4\times200p) + (1\times150p)}{5} =$	190p
200p	one for two	75p	$\dfrac{(2\times200p) + (1\times75p)}{3} =$	158.3p

Take the one-for-four rights at 150p, which gives an ex rights price of 190p. This is 5 per cent lower than the original market price of 200p, and is therefore the same result as if you had subscribed one new share at full market price (200p) and received a 5 per cent (one-for-twenty) scrip issue.

This 'scrip' element in the rights issue will be the difference between the pre-issue market price and the theoretical ex-rights price. If you are really thorough, and want to check your investment performance, you should record this factor against your original purchase price. If the ex-rights price is 190p against a pre-issue price of 200p, the original purchase price should be adjusted by multiplying by 0.95 (i.e., 190 ÷ 200). If the ex-rights price is 158.3, as in the alternative issue, then the 'scrip' factor is 158.3, ÷ 200 = 0.75.

This may seem rather unnecessary and tedious (I doubt whether many investors do it!). However, you should bear in mind that a 'deep discount' rights issue (i.e., an issue far below the market price) has rejigged the share books. If a company pays a maintained dividend per share after a rights issue at a big discount, it is effectively increasing the distribution on your new holding. And this increase is directly proportional to the 'ex rights factor'. Most companies do undertake to 'at least' maintain dividends in this way, so as to 'sweeten the pill' for shareholders.

Selling your rights

All this is what happens if you subscribe for new shares when a company makes a rights issue. But what if you do not want to put up the new money you are asked for? You might imagine that you could simply ignore the call: but you cannot normally do this, because if you do nothing at all, you will be left with your 'old' shares at a lower value. The normal best procedure is to sell your 'rights', in whole or in part. In the example I took of a one-for-four issue at 150p the value of these rights per share is, theoretically, the difference between the original pre-issue price (200p) and the ex-rights price of (190p). In this case it is 10p a share.

However, the form in which you must sell them is as a right to subscribe to the new shares-to-be. Since the proportion of the issue is one-for-four, the rights per share are multiplied by four (or whatever the proportion may be in different cases) to give the value of the right to subscribe to one new share.

'Allotment letters' can be sold

The procedure for rights issues is somewhat like that for scrip issues but with the extra choice of the 'rights' sale. You receive a proposal from the company; this is voted on, if necessary; you then receive allotment letters for the new shares. You may accept this, and subscribe, sending your cheque to the company before the appointed final date. If you do not want to subscribe, there is a period during which the allotment letters can be sold as the 'rights' to the new shares.

Your broker will guide you on the exact procedure and on the timetable for selling. The allotment letters are quoted just like a share. They are described as 'nil-paid' during the interim period before subscription. Their basic theoretical price is the difference between the subscription price of one new share (150p) and the final ex-rights price (190p), which is 40p in this case. This price is called the 'premium' for quotation purposes.

By selling your entire rights in this way, you will end up with assets to the same value as before the issue, though part of this will now be in cash: you had four shares at 200p (800p), and you finish with four shares at 190p (760p) plus 40p in cash. Note, however, that you have effectively reduced the value of your *holding* in the company.

If you want to keep this at the same level, and emerge without any cash, but without having to put up any new cash either, then you can sell just enough rights to cover the subscription to the rest. You would, of course, have slightly reduced your proportionate stake in the company. Again, your broker can easily work the sums out for you.

Stages of a rights issue — your choice on the way

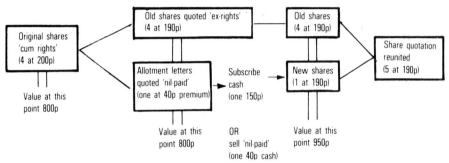

I should mention here that by selling your rights you will be making a 'disposal' for capital gains tax purposes, but without going into details at this stage, it is probably safe to assume that it will normally be a minor sum and covered by annual exemptions.

Some companies arrange for any rights not taken up, the 'rump', to be sold in the market if a premium can be obtained, on behalf of the non-subscribing shareholders. But this gives holders no control over the price at which the rights are sold, although it does avoid broker's commission.

All the calculations above make the assumptions that the shares of the company stay at the same market value during the period of issue. In real life this is not necessarily so.

First, the stock market as a whole may move up or down during the rights issue period. Second, the views of investors about the company, in particular, may be altered by the circumstances of the issue. If it is interpreted as a sign of weakness in the company's finances, it might cause a dip in the shares.

Rights issues always bring selling pressure

Whatever the opinion about the company, there are always shareholders who cannot take up new shares, particularly if the issue is proportionately a heavy one. So there will always be some sort of selling pressure on the shares. This may be matched up by optimistic buyers, but quite frequently it is not enough to stop a temporary decline in the price. This downward dip may well correct itself later, but during the period of issue it will affect the nil paid shares more sharply that the old shares.

The example, if the old shares drop from 200p to 180p then the ex-rights price would be 174p and the 'premium' of the 'allotment' letter will fall from 40p to 24p. Without going into exact calculations you can easily see how steep the gearing is on the 'premium' price by imagining a fall in the old shares to 150p, at which level the premium is zero.

Speculating in 'nil-paid'

Of course, this gearing of the nil-paid premium works both ways. A speculator, taking a bullish short-term view of the shares, may choose to buy the 'nil-paid' at a very low price in the hope of making a very large profit if the share price itself makes even a modest recovery. However this is not the first pre-occupation of the existing shareholder. He must decide what to do if the nil-paid get close to zero. So far as his original holding in the shares is concerned, the best advice is not to be panicked into selling at this stage. However, at very low levels of premium, there are virtually no 'rights' to be lost, so it is not necessary to do anything, and the rights can be allowed to lapse.

This extreme case, of shares falling down to, and indeed below the level of the new offer, is the fear which haunts companies and is the reason why most of their rights issues are 'underwritten'.

Underwriting the issue

Underwriting a share is a job which is done by the 'issuing house' to the company, usually a merchant bank in co-operation with one or more stockbrokers. An underwriter, for a fee, guarantees to take up the new shares if not enough are subscribed normally, and usually he will subcontract at least part of his risk to 'sub-underwriters'. There has always been a dispute as to the need for underwriting of rights issues. There is no doubt that a very deep discount on the offered shares, in no way affecting the efficiency of the operation, can eliminate all conceivable risks of market fluctuation in the old shares. My example earlier in this chapter, of a 'deep discount' of a one-for-two issue at 75p with the old shares at 200p, would avoid any likelihood of non-subscription. However, most companies still prefer to have underwriters for their own, strictly non-economic, reasons. There are also occasionally capital gains tax arguments against a 'deep discount' issue.

Vendor placings

Another type of equity issue has started to appear in the past year or so. This is the 'vendor placing'. Suppose your company acquires another company, and proposes to pay for it by a share issue. The 'vendor' (that is, the shareholder of the company being acquired) does not want to keep his new shares and these are therefore to be 'placed' with selected institutional shareholders of the acquiring company.

There obviously has to be an inducement for the institutions to take up these shares, so they are to be offered at a discount to the market price. Roughly like a rights issue, in fact, *except that all shareholders are not given the right to subscribe*. Depending on the size of the issue and the extent of the discount this can deprive the smaller shareholders of their capital. If your company should propose such a deal, it must, if it is sizeable, be put to shareholders. Refuse to vote for it, unless all shareholders are given an equal right to 'claw back' shares at the placing price from the original major participants.

21

Thrills and spills of the takeover

Investors holding shares in a company at the receiving end of a takeover bid can make large overnight profits. How do you spot the likely takeover targets? And how do you evaluate the bid terms?

Takeovers of one company by another are the events which above all others make the stockmarket headlines. This is natural, since they usually offer shareholders the same sort of quick gain as a horse-race or a pools win. That is, they offer it to the shareholders of the company being bid for because a bid will normally need to be above the market price of the shares. They may also bring a quick fall in the shares of the *bidding* company in some circumstances, or at least, they may reduce the performance of the shares of the bidder over a subsequent period.

As with a horse-race, the chances of becoming the beneficiary of a takeover are increased by the study of 'form', which in the stockmarket analogy is the knowledge of what industrial or other assets the company you think might be bid for possesses, how this relates to the share price, whether there is a powerful controlling shareholding, and so on. There are also some guidelines on the avoidance of investment in companies which in the past have indulged in large expensive purchases of other companies with little apparent benefit, and may therefore do so again.

In essence, both these sorts of appraisal are simply more concentrated forms of traditional investment criteria. Certainly, the identification of a takeover 'victim' is really the search for good value in the long term, such as a company which is perhaps run by dull managements, is going through a difficult patch, may have cut its dividend, and yet has a basically reasonable business. After that, the takeover itself is a matter of patience...and luck.

Don't hold non-voting shares
Rule number one, in any case (and whatever your investment aim), is not to buy non-voting shares. There are plenty of alternatives and if a takeover bid ever comes your way you *need* a vote. The question of share control by the directors of the company concerned, or their families, is of vital importance to the outcome of a bid, but it is not always a final barrier since families *can* differ amongst themselves and elderly company chiefs can be as tempted by high offers as any other holders. If you have the same sort of shares you can expect to get the same terms. But without a vote, you can't, and won't.

Takeover bids may take several forms, and as you will probably have observed from reading the financial press they can be very different in how they are played out. But the technical nature of most bids falls into three basic categories: cash; shares or other securities in the bidding company; or a mixture of both.

The significant difference between cash and securities is that taking cash for your holding is a disposal for capital gains tax purposes, whereas accepting securities is merely a continuance of your former holding in a different form. This in itself may influence your decision: I shall refer to the permutations on that theme later. Also, if you take cash you have no further interest in the fortunes of the merged group.

Types of securities offered

The securities offered by a bidder may simply be ordinary shares, or they may be another class of stock, such as convertible loan stock or convertible preference stock. These stocks are a form of deferred equity, offering an initial high fixed income but with an option to convert to shares later. The bid terms may also include a straight (non-convertible) fixed interest security.

Most bidders nowadays offer an underwritten cash alternative to their bid, even if it is primarily couched in terms of shares or other securities. This is effected by the merchant bank (or other agency acting as adviser to the bidder) undertaking to buy the new shares involved at a certain price. Needless to say, this is usually lower than the equivalent estimated value of acceptance of the shares, because it is not intended that the company should have to pay it: it is merely a form of guarantee of value, and/or a convenient selling opportunity for those wanting to accept cash (usually institutions which do not pay capital gains tax). It is therefore different from an actual cash bid, because the shares are all issued as though everyone had opted for them.

Cash attractions

If the bid is exclusively in cash then (aside from its intrinsic attraction or lack of attraction) the value to you is dependent on your capital gains tax liability. If you have no other gains tax liabilities, or likely liabilities, for the rest of the year, the normal annual exemption may cover this and you have a clear profit figure. The attraction of cash (again, ignoring for the moment the precise attraction of the terms) will also vary with your view of the stockmarket in general. If markets are going downwards and a cash bid continues to hold good, then it will have some sort of premium value over an equivalent current share value.

Uncertainties of a share offer

If the bid is purely in terms of shares of the bidding company, you will have a current market value to guide you, but a number of uncertainties thereafter. Apart from the general uncertainties of the market (it is going down, or up?) you have to recognise that the shares of a bidder may not stay at the same level once the bid is over.

Of course, the quality of the bidder's management and the way it handles its acquisition will ultimately be of great importance, but the arithmetic may point differently for a while. Much depends on the size of the acquisition and its cost to the bidder, as in the case of a rights issue.

Will the rating of the company that does the bidding subsequently be applied to the shares of the combined group? Or will the merged company be regarded as a totally new animal with a totally different investment rating? In practice the answer can vary considerably.

Let us take an example of a share offer. Suppose that Bidder, with a market capitalisation of £20m (20m shares at 100p each in the market) and a PE ratio of 10 as a rating (i.e., net earnings of £2m) makes an offer of one share for one of Victim.

If Victim has 10m shares, previously priced in the market at 50p, and a PE ratio of 5.0 on earnings of £1m, then the bid is an excellent deal for Victim's shareholders. But *how* excellent?

Simple arithmetic after the bid

Let us look at the simple arithmetic of putting Bidder and Victim together. The immediate total of earnings is £3m, up 50 per cent. The number of shares goes up to 30m, again 50 per cent.

So far as the nominal capital is concerned, this is in balance. But what about the price of the capital? If Victim's earnings were only worth a multiple of 5 before the bid, and Bidder is paying (by reference to its own rating) a multiple of 10, is the resultant mixture of earnings still going to be worth that same multiple? In other words, will the shares of the combined group command the same price as those of Bidder before the bid?

If the management of Bidder has achieved a deserved reputation for its 'dynamism' in its own business, you can assume that an improvement in Victim's profitability will follow a successful bid, and that therefore the eventual arithmetic will look better than our original £3m net earnings. But this will, at the least, take time.

If the stockmarket is going to give all the benefit of the doubt on this to the Bidder management, it *may* still value the enlarged company at the same share price as before, even if the improved profits are not yet in the bag. This will actually be a maintained rating. The real benefit will come if Bidder can improve Victim's profit trend, and thus keep a higher rating on the higher earnings. This is the thought behind all optimistic views on takeover bids. Such a development benefits both sides.

Possible exploitation of assets

A particular case where share improvement can sometimes be anticipated is where the net asset value of Victim is much higher than that of Bidder, and where these assets (if they are really underemployed, or realisable in some way) can generate higher returns eventually in Bidder's hands. If these assets are largely property and if Bidder is a skilled property manager, then the shareholders of both Bidder and Victim can benefit from the assets moving under Bidder's control via a takeover – provided the terms are fair.

This is one type of 'dynamic benefit' which used to be seen in the heyday of property booms. It can still apply, in certain conditions, where management is seen to be working effectively in this way.

'Reverse' bids and 'reluctant' bids

I ought to mention two special takeover cases where benefits from a higher share price can be expected, but without needing to exchange or sell your shares at all. First, the case where a successful private company is effectively merging with a quoted company by means of a 'reverse bid' (i.e., the quoted company makes a bid for the private one). The quoted company may have little to offer but cash and a quote, and its business will change completely with the injection of the private company, presumably for the better. So its shares can rise on the deal. Second, there is the case where an offer for shares in company XYZ is being made because the Takeover Code (referred to later) obliges someone who has built up a stake in XYZ to make it, but where the Bidder really does not want any more than his present holding. This is usually because he wishes to develop the company and also keep a good market in the shares.

You will need specific advice on both types of offer of course, since the character and reputation of the new managements in both cases are a vital key to the future progess of your shares.

Referring to my basic point however, you must consider, when looking at the share value of a proposed bid or merger, how big the acquisition is going to be for Bidder. In our example, the arithmetic of earnings and ratings (if the asset factor is ignored) will mean an uphill task for Bidder's share price.

Throughout the course of a bid, the debate is going to continue between the banks of Victim and Bidder, and in the columns of the press. The stockmarket will reflect general investment opinion. If there are no exceptional extra benefits to be seen from the bid (such as the consideration of asset value) then there is going to be some downward adjustment to Bidder's market share price.

Influences on the Bidder's share price
There will be several factors working on a Bidder's share price during a bid. First, as we have illustrated, there will be the sheer arithmetic, dictated by the relative size and cost. The smaller the victim, the less significance this has.

The second influence is the physical influence of buying in the market. Bidder's shares may be purchased by some investors with optimistic views of the company's outlook, in disregard of the immediate arithmetic. If it has a strong 'fan club', and powerful friends, this may keep the price higher than it might (or perhaps should) otherwise be. On the other hand there will be some investors looking at the arithmetic and pulling the other way. After the bid, if it is wholly in shares, there will be some selling by accepting holders of Victim who may not want all their new shares in Bidder. If there is a cash offer alternative to shares, the 'underwriters' of this cash offer may also be selling shares which they have taken on as a result of their commitment.

Finally, a balance will be struck and a settled new value will be established which will of course be modified much later by the demonstrated success or otherwise of the acquisition.

These are the underlying influences on the Bidder's shares, which will of course be interacting with those of the Victim whilst the bid is still on. Your most difficult choice as a Victim shareholder is to decide whether, at any stage, your shares are being overvalued as a result of all these influences, and whether this is significant enough to justify incurring a capital gains liability by selling your shares in the market rather than accepting the bid.

Ground rules for bids – the Takeover Panel
The ground rules for takeover bids are nowadays firmly established. They are contained in the City Code on Takeovers, and policed by the Takeover Panel. The Code is not a legal document and the Panel is not a legal body. But consisting as it does of senior representatives of the City, it has powers to make life very uncomfortable for transgressors; and it has greatly improved the position of the small shareholders in contentious bids.

The first risk to outside shareholders covered by the Code is that the bidder will secretly accumulate a powerful holding in the company he is pursuing. The Code cannot cover all the permutations possible over an extended period but it can and does control the sudden drive to acquire the victim's shares. Among various other requirements, all 'untoward' price movements in a company's shares must be reported to the Panel. If a bidder makes a 'dawn raid' (a single operation to acquire a large holding at one stroke from big institutional shareholders) then this must now be confined to 14.9 per cent of the shares in question, with a week's pause afterwards to allow outside shareholders time to assess the situation. Thereafter, the bidder can acquire further shares in the market, but when he reaches 30 per cent he must make a bid at a price not less than the highest price paid in the market over the previous twelve months.

There are numerous other rules concerning the accumulation of shares by one agency, or several acting together. They all aim at preserving the rights of all shareholders to equal treatment.

Selling before a bid
Your bid choices therefore may start before a bid, if you know that a large holding has been built up. Should you sell, if the share price has been driven to a tempting level, which it may well be during such a period?

If you decide not to sell, you run the risk that the imputed bidder will stop his holding at 29.99 per cent and then make no bid. However, this risk is usually worth running, since even if there is no immediate bid, it is rare for no further developments to take place. Of course, circumstances vary widely and you cannot be criticised for taking a handsome profit. But it is relevant that some stockmarket speculators actually buy shares at this or similar early stages in many bids hoping the ultimate profit will be greater.

Whether this pre-bid buying of shares goes on or not, you will, if an actual offer is going to be made, receive immediate news of this through an obligatory announcement, published in the press and also sent to you. This may or may not specify the terms of the offer but it will put you on guard – which is of course essential if the bid comes out of the blue.

The formal offer document – and afterwards
It may then be quite some time before the formal offer document is sent to you. This must, under the rules, contain all the details necessary for you to assess the value of the bid. If the bid is agreed by the board of your own company it will also contain a letter from them to this effect. If it is not agreed, then they will already have sent you instructions to do nothing, or to reject the bid. In a contested bid, there may well then follow a series of conflicting and perhaps increasingly acrimonious letters from each side.

You should not be in any hurry to make your commitment, even when at first the bid looks cut and dried, agreed by your company's board. There may well be another bidder, if your company's board seems eager to merge at too low a price. If your board is resolute, the bid may well be raised.

The formal offer document will specify the method whereby you should accept the bid and the final date for acceptance. If a bid is uncontested, or feebly contested, and runs the full course towards acceptance date without any rise in the market price above the estimated offer value, and no signs of an opposing bidder, then you are obviously in a poor position to refuse it. The acceptances received by the bidder must be published periodically through the period. When and if the bidder reaches acceptances of more than 50 per cent, he may declare the bid 'unconditional'. This means that he can and will keep the shares. This point may be reached before the final date.

Declaring a bid as unconditional is a point of strength for the bidder, and high acceptances should leave you with little option to refuse the bid. But it is still worth waiting until a late postal date before the final one before doing so. If you want to risk it, you can even go longer than that, because many bidders extend their 'last dates' and a genuine bidder is always glad to take further acceptances. There is a risk, however, in being left in a minority holding. If a bidder has gained more than 90 per cent of the shares he may, under company law, acquire the rest compulsorily. But if there are few profoundly dissenting holders, the bidder may only get, say, 85 per cent. Such a continuing minority holding is not likely to be rewarding. So don't risk going beyond the last date where acceptance otherwise looks inevitable.

Risk of Monopolies Commission
There is another risk, increasingly evident (usually at an earlier stage) in some bids. This is of a reference to the Monopolies Commission. Such a reference may prove unjustified but it can be made nevertheless, and it will hold up a bid for six months. It may cause the bidder to abandon the deal. There is no safeguard against this, except to keep in touch with all comment. If a reference looks likely, for obvious industrial reasons, you may care to sell the shares before it comes. But in any but this case, the risk is worth taking. A determined bidder will want to go ahead after the six months.

Watch the price behaviour
In all the complications of a bid you should pay attention to the behaviour of the market price. The latter may rise above the estimated bid value, and the press may indicate a possible rival bidder. Or the price may stay at a 'discount' to the bid value. This may, with a cash offer, be the natural discount on a delayed payment. With a share offer, it may indicate distrust of the bidder's 'paper' – i.e. a market reaction to the arithmetic I referred to earlier. If the market distrusts it, then *you* should think about it. You should certainly think hard about it if the 'paper' consists of a complicated double holding in preference shares or convertible loan stock. The 'aftermarket' in these might be very unsatisfactory.

In most normal bids, your position is much less ambiguous if your company is much smaller than the bidder: less chance of a 'reference' and a more assessable aftervalue for the shares. The moral in this case is certainly that smaller is beautiful!

22

New issues – how companies get a quote

There are now two types of new quotation possible. Here the main differences are explained

From time to time, entirely new issues of shares are brought to the stockmarket. In some cases, these may represent virtually new ventures, such as the new oil exploration companies referred to in my chapter on oil shares. But the rules of the Stock Exchange are such that only in special cases can a company start with a quotation for its shares in this way. Normally, companies have to present a history of several years trading, and be of a reasonable size, to get approval for an official quotation.

Reasons for 'getting a quote'

There may be many reasons why private or otherwise unquoted public companies seek a quotation on the Stock Exchange. There are two overriding ones, however: tax and/or growth. When the owner of a business built up over many years begins to think about providing for his family after his death, he may well decide to realise some of the value in his company by selling some of it to a wider public: and one of the ways of doing this is to reorganise the share capital and make a 'flotation' of the shares.

In many cases, the business concerned will also be expanding, and may have need of further capital other than that provided by ploughed back profits and bank borrowings. To keep a proper balance in this expansion, equity capital is essential, and a new share issue through the Stock Exchange is the best route for this.

The road to a Stock Exchange issue usually starts with the engagement of a financial advisor who can help with the often complicated changes needed in advance, and then with the operation of the issue. There are a number of such 'issuing houses': the leading houses are the well-known merchant banks which have for many years provided services of this kind. A Stock Exchange issue, however, also involves a stockbroker to cover the marketing of the shares; and some stockbroking firms undertake the whole operation without the agency of a merchant bank.

The Unlisted Securities Market

There are now two types of new quotation possible. In 1980, the Stock Exchange gave its approval to an entirely new form of share quotation, known as the Unlisted Securities Market (USM). This was established to accommodate smaller companies, or companies with a shorter trading record.

The regulations for the launching of these companies are not as strict as for an official 'listing'. The proportion of shares initially released to the market (i.e. not held by the original shareholders) need only be 10 per cent instead of the 25 per cent for a normal issue.

New issues on the USM have been plentiful since its establishment. However, by the nature of this method of flotation, the shares involved are likely to be in general less suitable for the small investor. When this market has a longer 'track record', and can be seen in better perspective, it should be possible to be more positive about it; but for the moment it ought to be for the more experienced investors, or those with a bigger existing spread of investments elsewhere. At any rate, if you do invest in a USM stock, you should be aware that it could carry a higher risk than an established larger company.

Quite apart from whether a company's shares are finally going to be quoted on the Stock Exchange or the USM, there are three main avenues towards a quote.

Introductions and placings

The most low-key of these is the 'introduction'. This may be arranged when the shares of the company concerned already have a wide ownership and an existing market. The most significant examples are the various foreign companies, large and well known in most cases and quoted already on the Stock Exchange of their country of origin, which have come to the London market in recent years. In these cases, the market-makers (i.e. the jobbers) have no problems in building up a London market; shares are always obtainable, and there will also be no undue extra demand.

The next degree up from this is the 'placing'. Here, shares really are issued to the public. The Stock Exchange expects at least 25 per cent of the company's capital normally to be sold to investors, of which a quarter goes to the jobbers to start the market off. But the issue is made, by the issuing house or broker, to selected clients. It is advertised, but in a relatively limited fashion since the size of such issues is likely to be small and too much enthusiastic interest might make the market in the shares a dangerous one for new buyers.

In both these cases the requirements in respect of the company's record and current circumstances are less onerous for the USM than for the Stock Exchange, though the continuing requirements (i.e. to keep shareholders informed of trading, and of all special matters of significance) are not too different.

Offers for sale

The form of new issue which is of most interest to the smaller investor, and in which he gets an equal chance of involvement along with the 'professionals', is the 'offer for sale', designed to obtain full listing on the Stock Exchange. Offers for sale may consist of entirely new shares, that is, the raising of new capital for the company concerned. Or they may represent the transfer of existing holdings (perhaps after a rearrangement of the capital) from old shareholders to the public. It is very often a bit of both.

It operates in the same way, whatever the source of the shares: the issuing house acquires them, and for a small margin of profit offers them to the public at a fixed price. Under conditions of very hectic activity in the new issues market there are periods where offers by 'tender' are also made, but this technique is not so often used for issues except where the likely market price is highly uncertain. The Government have also used it for some of the 'privatisation' issues, not always with success.

The offer is prominently advertised in the principal newspapers, each advertisement containing a detailed 'prospectus' covering the company's history, and its present circumstances, with all the facts and figures relevant for an assessment of the shares. It will also include an application form for anyone interested.

The requirements of the Stock Exchange are particularly strict with full offers for sale. A merchant bank, acting as the issuing house, has its own reputation to protect and will have taken pains to get to know the company well. Accountants will have investigated the figures thoroughly. In fact, the prospectus is often more informative as a single document than the regular annual reports from companies already quoted.

INTERPRETING THE PROSPECTUS

This is not to say that there are as *many* figures as in most sets of annual reports and accounts. In the latter many long-established companies give ten year records, with balance sheet details as well as profits and earnings details. A prospectus legally only needs to give profit records for five years, and in any case a relatively new company may not have a ten year record to put down.

But because of the independent accounting inspections, the records that *are* given will be more consistent and carefully vetted than may sometimes be the case with ongoing normal accounts. Moreover, you will get a picture of the company which is often more to the point than many of the details of the regular annual document. You should read this part of the prospectus even if you feel you need not bother about the rest.

Standard format of prospects

Prospectuses follow a standard format. First, there will be a section normally called **'History and Business'**. It will usually be readable and genuinely informative. Next will come a section on **'Management and Staff'**. It will give brief details of all the directors and other executives, details which may not be seen so clearly displayed again, since company law does not demand the publication of age and career record in any other sort of document. You can often get an extra insight into a company by looking at this simple background information. In many cases, with new issues, the board may be young, enterprising, with a wide range of experience; sometimes the senior directors may be near retirement, but this will be apparent, and so will the succession. (Would this were always as clear in the publications of established companies!)

There will then follow a section called **'Working Capital'**, which will confirm that the company has enough of this; but at this point there will also be an outline of how the issue proceeds (if new shares are being issued) will add to the company's resources.

Then follows the **'Accountants Report'**, containing the history of profits, and a balance sheet statement. This concludes with a section on **'Profits, prospects and dividends'**, where the directors usually give a forecast of the current year's profits, earnings, the dividends to be paid, and therefore the 'cover' for these payments.

The next, and usually the longest section is labelled **'Statutory and general information'**. This is the small print, containing amongst many other details the contracts entered into by interested parties, the shareholdings of the directors, and the details of how the issue has been arranged (including the costs).

Application for the issue

Finally, there will be the application form. Prospectuses are usually officially published on Mondays, and applications usually have to be lodged before 10am on the Thursday following. If the issue is an interesting or important one, there may well have been general comment on it by the press beforehand.

What should finally influence you? First you should note the general provenance of the issue: the status of the issuing house, the character of the company. In a big issue, this will be well understood in advance. Second, you should note the price of the offer, what the dividend yield, dividend cover and PE ratio will be on the forecast profit, all based on this price. Does this make the issue appear attractive?

There may be some easy comparisons to be made between the rating on the offer price with existing ratings of similar quoted shares (though bear in mind that existing share ratings, as published, will be on the last reported figures, not forecasts!). More often than not, comparisons will not be easy.

However, you may assume that the price will have been decided upon with a view to attracting subscribers. New issues are nearly all underwritten (that is, the issue is guaranteed to be taken up by a group of investment institutions, for a fee). But even so, no issuing house likes to risk a flop, for the sake of all the parties concerned. There are, from time to time, issues where the house concerned strikes a price which is considered pretty high. But normally, there will be a good margin between issue price and likely market price.

Where the offer is by tender, there will be no fixed comparison possible. Methods of structuring a tender offer vary. If you do fancy a tender offer, my advice is to study the press comment on the issue closely before making up your mind what price (or prices) to go for.

Another factor is: how many other competing offers have just been made, or are due to be made after the offer in question? There have been times when offers for sale were so plentiful that even reasonably attractive ones were 'crowded out' by bigger and more glamorous neighbours.

'Stagging' the offer

The reason for this is inherent in the tradition of the fixed price offer. Many people apply for such offers merely to sell the resulting shares in the market at a profit as soon as they know they have been successful. These are the 'stags' in stock exchange jargon. Many of them make multiple applications, committing a lot of their resources, of cash or bank overdraft, to make success more likely. The issuing house keeps all the cheques from an offer until everything has been sorted out. Thus there may not be enough 'stags' with enough money to go for the competing current offers.

You, too, can 'stag' an offer in this way if you wish. Issuing houses, when offers are oversubscribed, adopt various means to sort out applicants. Small applicants are sometimes favoured with full acceptance, with larger ones being scaled down. When huge oversubscription occurs, a ballot is inevitable for all applicants but small one may get better chances. This is why it can pay to put in a number of applications. But there is no rule for success when an offer is very popular.

If you do succeed, you will get back a renounceable allotment letter. This contains instructions for selling, which you may then wish to do (consulting your broker) on the first dealing day after the issue.

Or, on the other hand, you may wish to keep the shares if you like the company. Quite often, shares in a popular issue may make a very confused market in first dealings, take some time to settle down, then continue to rise. Some market professionals use the first dealings, when stags are selling, to pick up shares which they consider cheap. So it could pay you to wait: following the old rule of doing the opposite of the 'crowd'. In the case of British Telecom, those who continued to hold their shares throughout the months after the offer made far more than the 'stags', and were able to sell at leisure if they wished, taking a cooler view.

23

More about gilts – and other fixed interest stocks

I would personally prefer to define an 'investment' as something which stood a chance of 'real' growth over the years (in other words, growth over and above the rate of inflation). In most senses conventional gilt edged stocks, and other fixed interest securities, are not in this category. But as I pointed out in my earlier chapter on gilts, they are certainly likely to appreciate in value in real terms if inflation declines (and does not accelerate again), over the next few years.

Meanwhile, conventional gilts have features which some investors find attractive or useful. The first of course is that of high current income, relative to most shares. This is of most appeal to basic-rate or otherwise low taxpayers. The second is that repayment, at a guaranteed price, may often afford a capital profit. Gilts do not attract capital gains tax on a sale or 'redemption'. So this feature is particularly attractive to high taxpayers.

A purchase of gilts does not attract Stamp Duty and commission costs are also very low, particularly if you buy through the Post Office (which keeps a list of acceptable stocks for this method of purchase).

Wide permutations of redemption date and 'coupon'
The dates of redemption of the many government stocks vary from under one year to well over twenty years ahead, with a few stocks (the irredeemables) which do not have any repayment date.

The 'coupon' rates also vary, from 2½ per cent up to 15½ per cent. The combination of redemption and coupon creates many permutations of income and capital return. Naturally enough, stocks with low coupons offer less income (bearing tax) and proportionately more in capital return. Because of their appeal to high taxpayers they are often priced in the market at levels which are only of interest to those taxpayers and not to 'basic rate' investors.

Taking actual examples, slightly simplified, shows how the market works, and the returns involved. (Of course, the prices and thus the returns will be out of date as you read this, but the principles remain the same.) Let us start with a very 'short' stock. On one particular date, Exchequer 3 per cent 1984 was priced at £80. It yielded 3.7 per cent gross in current income. (£3 on £777 as a percentage.) It offered 25 per cent capital appreciation on redemption at £100 in three years from the date of purchase. So, after income tax at 50 per cent, you were offered a net return of 1.85 per cent (after tax) each year on income, and about 8½ per cent per annum equivalent for three years, with no tax. So your total annual return would have been 10.35 per cent net, equalling 20.7 per cent if you had held a fully taxable deposit and paid income tax at, say, 50 per cent.

The same sort of arithmetic works for other low coupon stocks. The further the date of redemption, the lower the price. Transport 3 per cent 1988 was, at the same time, £60 or so, yielding about 5 per cent on income. It offered 66 per cent capital appreciation over seven years, equal to about 8½ per cent per annum. Add the 'net' annual income (2½ per cent) and you had roughly the same return.

At the other end of the coupon scale, we had Treasury 15 per cent 1985 standing at £97.50, yielding 15.4 per cent on income and offering virtually no capital appreciation.

Corporation stocks and company debentures
As well as government stocks, there are also corporation (city and local authority) issues, for those who want a somewhat higher income.

Even higher annual yields are offered by the debentures and other loans of industrial and other companies. The variation here is of course very wide, depending on the ranking and security of the stock, the status of the company, and the terms and size of the issue. The highest ranking company loan stock is the debenture. This is a loan which is secured by a mortgage on property owned by the company. In a liquidation it therefore gets paid before all else (except the tax man). Below this in ranking come loan stocks, some secured on company assets, some unsecured. The security of any debenture or loan is obviously less in practice if the company is not in good health, or has doubtful assets.

Debentures or secured loans rank before all creditors (except for the tax man). Unsecured loans do not rank before creditors, however. They take their place with these for the shareout.

'Cover' for capital and interest
As well as a high capital cover, a loan should have an adequate cover for its interest. 'Cover' is based on profit before tax, minus any payments on a prior charge loan. Moreover, with an unsecured loan, there should be some assurance that the company cannot issue unduly large amounts of new loan standing 'pari passu' (i.e., holding similar rights) with the existing loan.

From the investment angle, a well secured loan stock with a company of a good standing will usually yield more than gilt-edged stock. But there is no exemption from capital gains tax on sale profits. Nor is the market in many loan stocks as easy as in gilts, though this will not normally be a hindrance to a small investor.

From the company's angle, the issue of loan stock has often been attractive in the past, when interest rates were lower. The average company's profit growth has been well above the rate of interest paid. Interest on loan stocks is deductable before corporation tax: this, at current rates of tax, effectively halves the servicing cost. As I write, interest rates are high enough to discourage many new issues. Also, such is the number of allowances on capital and current spending, that not all companies pay corporation tax. But conditions may change.

Preference shares – how they differ from loan stocks

Preference shares are fixed interest, like loan stocks. They are not company liabilities, however, but share capital. In other words, they have no ranking, for capital repayment or income, ahead of any creditor. They only rank ahead of ordinary shares. Payment of preference dividends is made on the same basis as on ordinary shares: it is paid net, after deduction of basic rate income tax, paid by the company as Advance Corporation Tax (ACT).

The forms of adding security for preference stocks include making them 'cumulative' (i.e., if the dividend is passed in any one year, it has to be paid up later when profits allow this) and sometimes 'redeemable' (i.e., the stock has a finite life, and may sometimes offer a bonus on redemption).

Clearly, however, preference has much less security than loan, and yields are usually higher. There are some advantages for low taxpayers who can reclaim the 'tax credit' (i.e., the deducted tax) on preference dividends.

CONVERTIBLES – FIXED INTEREST WITH EQUITY

A 'convertible' is a fixed-interest stock, issued by a company, which carries the right to convert into ordinary shares of that same company at some future date. The form of fixed-interest stock varies. It may be a debenture or a secured or unsecured loan. Or may be a preference stock. Most convertibles are based on unsecured loan stocks, but preference issues have been popular from time to time.

When issued, the stock will of course have a fixed 'coupon' (or dividend) and will usually have a conventional date for redemption (about twenty years or so after issue). It will also have the right to convert into so many shares at a certain date in the future. The conversion date is normally much earlier than that of redemption. Modern convertibles have quite an extended period for conversion (though usually with only one day in each year for the exercise of this choice).

Once a convertible has been issued, it will settle into some sort of pattern of value in the market, depending on the views of investors about the company and its shares (views which can of course change).

Coupon and yield

The coupon of the stock will probably be lower than on a straight fixed-interest issue. So will the yield, if the underlying equity is judged attractive. Let us suppose that the yield on a straight loan stock would be 12½ per cent. Thus, one might see a 10 per cent convertible loan, of company ABC, redeemable in 1999, standing at £100 in the market to yield 10 per cent with the ordinary shares of the company yielding 5 per cent at 400p each.

Value of conversion

Suppose also that conversion was at the rate of 20 shares for each £100 nominal of the stock, and the conversion option first exercisable in five years' time. There is now another figure to reckon on: conversion, in terms of the current ordinary share price, is worth £80 (i.e., 20 × 400p). Since the convertible stock is actually 25 per cent higher than this in the market, it is said to have a 25 per cent 'premium' on conversion.

The size of this premium, and thus the current yield on the stock, depends on how attractive eventual conversion is expected to be. Clearly, in this case, there is expectation of reasonable growth from the share, enough to cover the 'premium'. So this is the current market 'price' exacted from the investor for the benefit he is getting now in the shape of higher immediate income.

This is the sort of market approach towards shares with reasonable growth prospects which leads to the issue of convertibles. In these terms they are a compromise between future growth expectations and current income. Of course, a high-rate taxpayer is unlikely to be interested in such stocks. If he liked a company's prospects enough, he would want to buy the ordinary shares.

But there are enough of the other kinds of investor to create demand for convertibles. Most prominently, there are the pension funds and other trusts which pay no income tax. However, the private investor on basic or medium-rate tax may also see some advantages, which I will refer to later.

Motives for issuing convertibles

The reasons why companies issue convertibles are more or less a reflection of the investment demand for them. The company wants to offer a higher immediate income than on its ordinary shares, but does not wish to incur the whole immediate cost of interest on a straight loan stock. (Companies also get relief from corporation tax on loan interest, anyway, though on preference stocks they pay basic rate tax to the Revenue.) A typical occasion for the issue of a convertible is when a highly rated company (i.e., one with a low current yield on its shares) is making a takeover bid for a lower-rated one. The capital value of the bid must be an attraction to ensure acceptance, but a straight share offer might result in a reduction in income for accepting shareholders. Instead, a convertible stock can be arranged to give parity or superiority of immediate income to accepting investors.

Fall-back against bad luck

The compromise represented by a convertible is not always entirely involved with whether you pay tax at a high rate on income. You may wish to hold a convertible because, since no company's growth can be entirely certain, you want some basic insurance against future bad luck in its business. A very poor performance in the shares would be mitigated in the convertible by its basic fixed interest properties.

This is not the sort of expectation behind any investment decision, but it may be another way of looking at the 'compromise' of a convertible which you should think about.

There *are* convertibles which have more or less reached this stage of fixed interest, after a long-period of poor performance by the shares. The conversion date has either passed or (such is the price of the shares) the stock is never likely to be worth converting. In the latter case, the yield on the convertible will be as high as on an equivalent pure fixed interest stock, but the conversion premium will also be very high. In some small issues of this kind, the income can be attractive to those that want it, simply because the stock is 'friendless'.

Where the 'pull' of the share is strongest

At the other end of the scale from these 'failed' convertibles there are others where, with conversion near at hand, the attraction of the share is such that conversion is inevitable. In these cases, there will be no conversion premiums; in fact, there will usually be a discount. And the yield on the stock will be correspondingly low. There will, in other words; be no advantage in buying the convertible except as a substitute for the share.

Suppose our company, ABC in the earlier example, had progressed for five years and the first conversion date was near. Suppose dividends had grown by 15 per cent each year, therefore doubling. Suppose also that the shares still yielded 5 per cent (i.e., that they had also doubled). So, conversion would be worth £160 (800p × 20). If the market price of the convertible, at this stage, exactly matched the terms of conversion, the stock would stand at £160, so the yield would be 6.2 per cent (i.e., the £10 coupon on £160). The market price would probably be a bit lower in practice, as there tends to be a natural discount on any future event, however certain.

ABC shares: price 400p: yield 5%. ABC convertible: price £100: yield 10%.
Can convert into 20 ABC shares per £100 in five years' time.
TWO INVESTMENT PROFILES AFTER FIVE YEARS

	Share dividends grow at 15% per annum, price rises in proportion			*No growth in share dividends, share price halves over period*		
	Price	Yield	Total return at 5 year stage*	Price	Yield	Total return at 5 year stage
Share	800p	5%	+115%	200p	10%	−37½%
Convertible	£160	6.2%	+85%	£80**	12.5%	+5%

* Approximate figures, assuming 50% tax on income. ** Assuming that this would be a fixed interest yield. Price depends on level of interest rates. Actual conversion price with shares at 200p would be £40.

My first 'scenario' (the growth one) in the table shows that you would have done better over these five years in the shares. But, your return on the convertible would not have been all that bad. Of course, if you can be certain of the share growth or are prepared to take the risk (which is a perfectly reasonable equity investment attitude) then the shares are for you. Indeed, it would be a mistake to buy the convertible on these terms. But my example is pure hindsight, and you may feel like having the insurance a convertible gives. My second scenario in the table illustrates how this might work! The shares prove a disappointment and their price falls. For the convertible holder, the option to convert likewise falls: but the straight fixed interest return (whatever that might at the time) acts as a support.

24
Warrants, options and traded options

If convertible stocks are for those who prefer their equity investment with a higher immediate income, or with reduced share risks, there are certain other specialised forms of investment which suit those who want to avoid income altogether. But they must be willing to increase their 'exposure' to share movements for the chance of higher capital profit.

WARRANTS

These are, in essence, the right to purchase a specific share, at some future date or dates, at a set price. Years ago, they arose as another method of issuing a loan stock with an added equity attraction: rather like a convertible. But in many of these loan stocks the warrant element was detachable, and subsequently acquired a quotation of its own in the market.

The price of a warrant in the market depends on the usual complex interaction between all the factors of dates and prices mentioned above. A recent example, of a warrant in the shares of an investment trust, will illustrate some of the permutations. The share price is, say; 86p. The warrant is to subscribe at 70p for the shares, after publication of the annual accounts in any year up to six years from now, and the warrant price itself is 35p. So the life of the warrant is reasonable. Short lives are less useful because they limit the 'play' in the price. You will note that in this case there is an immediate positive difference (of 16p) between the 'exercise' price and the share price. This is called the 'intrinsic value' of the warrant.

In this case, there is also a 'premium' over the 16p intrinsic value of 19p. This is the cost to you of buying the advantage of the warrant over the share (sometimes there is no intrinsic value and then the warrant price will of course be entirely premium).

What are these advantages which you pay for? Well, the warrant price is much less than that of the share. So you can obtain all the capital appreciation in the share, over the exercise price, for a fraction of the outlay. In this case the share price is 2.5 times that of the warrant. This is known as the 'gearing'.

The premium is what you pay for this advantage, looking at the warrant over its whole term. To justify the warrant price, the share, firstly, has to rise by 19p (which is 22 per cent or about 3 per cent per annum). It also has to compensate for the dividend you are losing by buying the warrant rather than the share, though against this you can offset the notional interest saving from the lower capital outlay. After this, the premium will look 'cheap'.

However, the attraction of warrants to the speculator is that the premium tends to remain in existence in the short term however the share price moves. This is where the gearing comes in. If, as in the diagram, the shares were to rise by this 19p in the space of a few months, the warrant could be expected to rise by not much less than this. You can see that a 22 per cent rise in the share equals a rise of 53 per cent in the warrant (19p on 35p), if the premium were to remain unchanged. It won't entirely do so, because the 'intrinsic value' is going to rise and thus the future potential will be less and 'cost' becomes cheaper. But even so, the percentage profit on the warrant will be substantially more than on the share.

The reverse is also the case. You would lose more on the warrant if the share price dropped. For this reason you need to be very sure that the share itself is basically 'cheap', or attractive in its own right, before venturing into the warrant. You need professional advice or a lot of experience in spotting such situations.

How the 'gearing' of a warrant can work over the short term

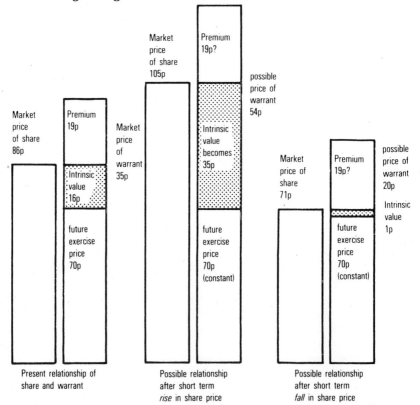

OPTIONS (NON-TRADED VARIETY)
The same point applies to options. These are contracts, giving you the right to buy or sell a specific share at a specific price at a future date. One difference between options and warrants is in the word 'sell'. You can take a bullish or a bearish view with an option. Another difference is that traditional (non-traded)

options can only be exercised at one date, and that date may not exceed three months after the contract.

The third difference is that options are a contract, and they are not in themselves a quoted 'piece of paper'. We will deal later with traded options, which are quoted, but at the moment we are looking simply at the contract itself.

The fourth difference is that options are theoretically obtainable in any share and certainly so in all the market leaders.

Options are purchased for a percentage of the underlying share price, which varies according to the 'volatility' of the share, i.e., whether it is more or less extreme in its fluctuations. You can see the rates quoted on leading stocks on the prices pages of the *Financial Times*. Currently, they vary from 6 to 12 per cent.

You can purchase an option either for the 'call' (the right to buy the share) or the 'put' (the right to sell it) or a double option (to buy or sell it). The latter, of course, costs roughly double the rate of the single option. The period will be fixed, with the three month maximum obviously the best choice in most cases. The exercise price is called the 'striking price', and it will be based on the current market price of the share, plus (in the case of call options) an extra percentage to cover the borrowing costs, on the funds involved, by 'the market'.

The particular feature of options unobtainable in warrants, is the ability to speculate on the fall of the shares concerned, over a period long enough to be useful, and without exposure to unlimited loss. You cannot lose more than your option money.

You can use options in conjunction with dealings in the actual shares, as an insurance against a wrong decision. This is, in effect, the reverse of speculation, and we shall have more to say on this, when looking at traded options.

TRADED OPTIONS

A traded option, like the conventional option contract, gives the right to buy or sell a particular share at a pre-established price over a given period. An option to buy a share is known as a 'call' option, and one giving the right to sell a share is known as a 'put' option.

The big difference between the traded option and the conventional one is that the traded option can, itself, be bought and sold almost as if it were a share. This means that even if you guess wrong about the movement in the price of a share in which you buy a traded option you could decide to cut your loss and sell rather than inevitably losing the whole of your 'premium' – the price you pay for the option.

The traded options market operates from one of the pitches on the floor of the Stock Exchange in London and has 'marketmakers' much like the market in shares. These 'marketmakers' are in fact normally firms who operate in shares as well.

Traded options are currently available in the shares of a number of major quoted companies, giving a pretty representative spread of different types of stock. The oil giants, Shell and BP are there, as is chemical giant ICI. Barclays represents the clearing banks, resource stocks include Consolidated Gold, RTZ and Vaal Reefs, and there are household names of British business such as Courtaulds, GEC and Marks & Spencer.

Prices of traded options are quoted in the Stock Exchange's daily official list, but details of those most recently traded can be obtained daily from the *Financial Times* under the heading of 'London Traded Options'. A glance at this list will help in understanding the market.

The left-hand column gives the name of the underlying stock with the current market price of the ordinary shares.

A range of 'exercise' prices
The next column gives the 'exercise price' – the price at which the option confers the right to buy or sell the relevant share. For most of the shares a range of options exercisable at different prices is quoted. In a copy of the *Financial Times* on one particular date we would have seen call options in BP exercisable at 260p, 300p, 320p and 330p, and put options exercisable at 240p, 300p, 320p and 330p. The BP share price at that time stood at 300p.

The next thing we see is that, for each exercise price, options are available expiring at three different dates: in the case of BP these were at that time January, April and July.

When an option expires, a new one is created. Thus the BP Januaries will expire as each January closes but a new class of BP October options will be created. New options series are also created when the underlying share price moves significantly: the idea is that there should always be at least one option available above the current share price and at least one below.

'In' and 'out' of the money
A call option exercisable at a price above the current share price is known as 'out of the money'. If the exercise price is below the current share price, the option is called 'in the money'. If exercise price and share price are the same – as was the case in our example for the BP 300s – the option is 'at the money'. But remember that with put options (giving the right to sell the shares) the position is reversed: With BP at 300p, a BP 240 put option is 'out of the money' and a BP 320 put option is 'in the money'.

There are a couple more technical points we need to note where the traded option market differs from the market in shares. First, all deals are for cash – there is no account system. Second, you cannot buy an individual option – all deals are for one or more 'contracts' of 1,000 options each. So an order to your broker might go 'buy me two contracts in BP April 320 call options at 11p' and the value of the deal excluding costs would be a total of £220.

Options strategies: 'writing' options
Without going into detail, it can be appreciated that the market can be used in two totally separate ways: to increase risk by increasing 'gearing' or to decrease risk by writing call options – and there are many other strategies which arise in between.

The 'writer' of an option is effectively the other side of the transaction in which an investor buys an option. A holder of BP shares might, say, take the view that they were more likely to fall than rise over the next seven months, and that even if they rose he would be quite happy to sell if he could get 330p for them. If he then 'writes' a BP 330 July call option at 11p premium, he gets an immediate 11p per share which he pockets. If he is right and the options expire worthless, that is the end of the matter. If he is wrong and the BP price rises to the point where he is 'exercised' he still sells the shares at 330p which, together with his 11p premium, means that effectively he has got 341p for them.

The buyer's strategy

For the buyer the appeal of options is that they are much cheaper than the underlying shares and he can thus take a view on the market or an individual share at much reduced cost. In the case of BP 330 April call options, the 11p he pays is all 'time value' – the option is 'out of the money' and will have no 'intrinsic' value unless and until the BP share price rises above 330p. At expiry date it will need to have risen above 341p before he can show an overall profit on the transaction. However, in general most buyers of options aim to make quick profits, and have usually sold before expiry date.

But if, say, he buys a BP 260 April call option at 48p, as much as 40p of that premium is already 'intrinsic' value with the shares at 300p. The remaining 8p is time value; the price paid for the chance the BP share price may rise further during the life of the option. The longer an option has to go before expiry, the higher the time value will normally be. But remember that this time value must erode to nothing by the exercise date of the option. If you hang on you only make money if the underlying share price (and therefore the intrinsic value of the option) rises faster than the rate the time value erodes.

'At the money' call options in particular can show very large percentage rises for a small rise in the underlying share price. It can, of course, go the other way and in this sense options are a high-risk investment, except that maximum losses are limited to the premium paid, which is at least considerably less than the cost of the underlying share.

The FTSE 100 Index and the Futures Contract

Another form of contract in the traded option market has followed the establishment of a new market index. This is the so-called "FT SE 100 Index". It consists of 100 leading stocks, which makes it almost as good a reflection of general market movements as the FT Actuaries All Share Index. The important difference is that the FTSE 100 Index is recalculated every minute during Stock Exchange trading hours. It is therefore just as tradable as a share.

On this basis, the FTSE 100 Index is in fact used now as a vehicle for an option, subject to the same rules as for the shares in the option list.

A more fundamental use of the FTSE 100 Index has been devised. This is the Futures Contract, and is not traded on the Stock Exchange but in the London International Financial Futures Exchange ('LIFFE' for short). In principle it resembles the sort of contract effected in commodities of various kinds. Somewhat like an option, it is not a purchase or sale of an asset but an obligation to accept or make delivery at some later date. Of course, since an Index cannot be physically bought or delivered, there is a unit of cash calculated instead, based on the FTSE 100 Index price at the appropriate time. The Futures Contract is purchased 'on margin' – that is, your commitment is only a fraction of the full 'unit price' of the Index. If you are interested, your broker will provide you with details of the rules. These are quite different from those involved in share buying – and this is a market where very large gains or losses are possible, so make sure you know exactly what you are doing before taking action.

25

Investing the unit trust way

Unit trusts are an indirect way into share investment for investors who wish to achieve a wider spread of risk than they could do with the funds at their disposal by buying shares direct, or who want to avail themselves of professional management.

A unit in a unit trust is not a share, though it reflects everything that happens to the shares in the unit trust's portfolio, in both capital and income. In this respect it is different from the shares in an investment trust, whose prices move as they are bought and sold in the market.

Trustees and managers

Each unit trust is set up by a trust deed, an agreement between the trustees (usually one of the big banks) and the manager of the fund concerned. The deed has to be approved by the Department of Trade and embodies all the regulations and procedures laid down by the Department in great detail.

The trustee is not responsible for the choice of investments. That is the manager's job. The management company is responsible for all the investment and administrative tasks in the running of the trust. The trustee, however, is the legal holder of all the funds involved, and literally acts in trust for the unit holder.

The strict regulations of unit trusts arose in the first place because a unit trust can advertise and take in money from investors at large. Indeed, this was the aim of unit trusts when first formed: to channel funds into equity investment.

The Government regulations apply to 'authorised' unit trusts. Funds managed from outside the UK (offshore funds) are not 'authorised'. They are not allowed to advertise in the UK but nor are they regulated.

Buying and selling units

You can buy a unit trust unit by getting directly in touch with the management company of the fund in question by writing or telephoning, with a simple form to complete the transaction. The same applies to selling. The names and addresses of all the management groups, with their funds and the current prices for these, can be found in the pages of the *Financial Times* and other newspapers.

When you buy units, your money normally increases the size of the fund. The trust is designed to cope with the inflow (and outflow) of money by dividing the value of all the investments and cash it holds by the number of units in existence every day (or at some other regular interval); this gives a value for the individual units.

Sometimes managers can match buyers and sellers of units without adding to or subtracting from the underlying investments the trust owns. If necessary managers must create new units to accommodate demand, and must 'liquidate' units to cope with outflow. In practice, managers keep a 'float' of existing units which accommodates buying and selling on a routine basis. A fund which is steadily growing, however, will need to create new units from time to time, and one which is steadily shrinking will need to liquidate units on the same basis. Moreover, there may be sudden periods of excess demand (such as a sudden speculative interest in a specialised trust, or a market 'panic') where the buffer stocks of units prove inadequate.

Pricing of units, and charges

The pricing of units is laid down by Department regulation. It starts with the prices of the shares the trust owns as they are quoted in the market, with an offer price (higher, for buying) and a bid price (lower, for selling). The valuation of these prices, divided by the number of units, produces a crude offer and bid price for the units themselves. These are adjusted for dealing costs, for stamp duty and for the initial management charge to buyers of units. Initial charges vary, 5 per cent being usual now (the Department of Trade used to regulate charges, but no longer does so, though any charges have to be approved by unitholders in meeting).

The total effect of the official method of pricing would give a very wide spread, more than 13 per cent. But because the managers can absorb normal selling through the float of units, the typical spread of prices is around 7 per cent or so. In a growing fund, this will normally be the spread from the *offer price downwards*. But in a shrinking fund the spread will usually be from the *bid price upwards* (which is known as the 'liquidation basis'). A move from the offer basis to the liquidation basis can occur in times of sudden selling, as referred to above. It creates a drop in the unit price quite unconnected with the underlying value.

This is something to watch for. You can always find out, in any instance, from the managers, if this has happened. Then, if you are a potential seller, you may do better to wait until the offer basis has been restored. Of course, if you are a buyer you then have a temporary advantage in your purchase price. The Department of Trade has proposed a different method of unit pricing which does not involve the bid and offer spread, but takes pricing from a mid-point quote, upwards and downwards. However this will still involve large shifts upwards or downwards to accommodate changes in demand as described above.

Apart from this risk of switches in pricing, the total buying and selling costs of a unit trust investment are therefore considerably lower for small sums than for dealings in shares as such. While the investment is held there is also an annual management fee. Typically, this is ½ per cent, which comes out of income and is therefore a deduction for tax purposes.

One advantage which both unit trusts and investment trusts now possess is their exemption from capital gains tax on their own dealings in the securities the trust owns. The unit holder is liable to CGT on a sale of units at a profit but he has the index-linked annual exemption to play with (see later chapter on CGT).

Choosing a trust
There are a daunting number of trusts to choose from, and these consist of several different types. First, and most numerous, are the 'general' trusts, with a wide spread of shares, very often mainly in the UK market, with the aim of giving a balance between capital performance and income. Then there are trusts specifically oriented to growth in capital, with little emphasis on income. There are also trusts (whose number has increased in recent years) who aim is to provide a higher than average initial yield, and also to seek annual growth in income as a primary target.

Some trusts may specialise in certain share sectors, such as commodity shares, or financial shares. A most important form of specialisation is in overseas markets, where there are trusts invested in most of the principal areas.

The type of trust you select will involve the same decisions you have to make on shares: degrees of risk and hopes of reward, timing in purchases and sales. Clearly, specialised (and particularly overseas oriented) funds can be more profitable if the timing of your deals is right. But the risks of getting it wrong are high.

'High yield' funds
There is also a place for a 'high yield' fund, which is not specialised in the normal sense of the term, for investors who want or need income but don't want to lose the prospect of capital and income growth as they would in some savings deposits.

The best way to sort out the choices available, both in types of funds and in management groups, is to study one or other of the specialised journals dealing with the field, such as *Money Management* or *Planned Savings*. Background information and details of unit trusts can also be found in *The Unit Trust Year Book* (Financial Times Business Information). And, as always, keep reading the financial press for trends and comments. Your stockbroker will certainly help you with final selections but you need to acquire the background before reaching this stage.

PERSONAL EQUITY PLANS
In his 1986 Budget, the Chancellor introduced a new concept for individual investors, taking effect from January 1987. This was the 'Personal Equity Plan', or PEP. His idea was to encourage the smaller investor (by means of tax reliefs) into direct shares in the companies of their choice, rather than simply opting for unit trusts.

The basics of PEPs are that you may invest up to £2,400 per year in listed and USM companies, and that provided the sums involved stay invested for at least one complete calendar year, the proceeds will be free of income and capital gains tax. The £2,400 maximum may be accumulated over any calendar year on deposit, and then invested in a lump sum towards the end: provided it is invested within the calendar year it qualifies for the tax relief. Unit trusts or investment trusts may be used for part of the scheme, but the main investment must be direct into shares.

After this first calendar year of 'build-up' in the investments, the scheme must run for another full calendar year before qualifying. It may then either be terminated, or allowed to run on. Each year a new scheme may be started, but only one scheme per year is allowed. After the qualifying period is reached in any scheme (i.e. two calendar years of operation and at least a year and a day of investment) that qualifying scheme may be amalgamated with any other qualifying schemes to form a unified portfolio.

The PEPs must be undertaken through Plan Managers, who have to be authorised to administer them. Most stockbrokers, and many unit trusts management groups, will be offering schemes. Out of the £2,400 maximum, up to £600 may be put into unit or investment trusts. However, if unit or investment trusts are exclusively used (with no share investment) then only £420 per year is allowed.

Clearly, PEPs are an attractive option for many investors, particularly for high tax payers. But they have their snags. The first is that, with all the complications of running them, the managers' charges are going to be fairly high. For small investors, without existing equity investments, they could also be rather risky in their early stages, since £2,400 is not going to give much of a spread of investment. A really adequate spread will involve even higher costs of dealing, and that could eliminate a lot of the tax benefit. If you are a really small investor, you could be better off by sticking to a pure unit trust version, investing only the £420 lump sum, or accumulating at £35 per month. You could, for exmaple, make the most of the tax relief by putting your money into a high income fund.

If you are prepared for more risk than this, then you could stick to very sizeable leading companies, two or three to start with. If you continue to take new schemes out, the risk will of course reduce with time as you gather new constituents for your portfolio. But do find out before you start what the total level of charges is going to be.

26

Insurance-linked investment – the pros and cons

One of the advantages of unit trust investment is that you can buy or sell small numbers of units easily and economically. Arising out of this it becomes possible to make regular small purchases of units on, say, a monthly basis, at an economic cost. You thereby also obtain one form of investment advantage – of spreading the risk of wrong timing.

Regular premium schemes
You undertake a scheme like this by buying unit trust units direct. But you can also do it through the medium of an insurance policy. For in practice unit-linked life assurance is similar to unit trust investment. The main difference is that a small proportion of the money you put up goes to buy the life assurance benefit. The remainder is invested in 'units' in a portfolio of investments, and the value of your investment fluctuates in line with the value of these units. The mechanics of such a regular savings plan are as follows: the monthly premiums go largely into units of your choice with only a small element (often 5 per cent, but rising with age) going towards actual insurance. For this you get only a limited guaranteed sum. You also, of course, pay management charges on the investment content. If you had taken out a policy before 13 March 1984 you would receive income tax relief on your premiums, to offset these charges. However, since that date, new policies have ceased to obtain tax relief.

Tax differences with insurance funds
Thus you no longer get a 'discount' on your purchase of units. Moreover, your investment performance is reduced by capital gains tax, which the fund has to pay. Unit trusts do not have to pay this on profits earned within the fund, and you as an individual can use your annual index-linked exemption to avoid or mitigate the effects of capital gains tax when you sell your units. But an insurance fund (which is what a linked policy is) is liable to CGT.

As with any other insurance policy, there may be a surrender penalty if you cash in too early. You also lose the benefit of the premium tax relief (on policies taken out before 13 March 1984) if you stop the scheme before the fourth year, partially losing it, in downward steps, until the tenth year (most schemes are of this length).

So a unit-linked scheme is mainly useful for longer-term savings and compares best with the direct unit trust method if you are a high taxpayer, keeping a close control over your tax affairs.

As always, the really important factor is how well the underlying fund is managed. Compared to this the method of the investment is secondary.

Single premium bonds

This universal rule applies equally to the other main form of insurance-linked investment, known as the 'single premium bond' or 'investment bond'. This is a lump sum investment which is technically a single premium insurance policy.

As such, a small amount of the money goes into actual insurance, the rest (after an initial fee) goes into an investment fund of your choice. As an insurance fund it is liable to CGT. When a bond is cashed, there is no individual CGT payable, but the whole 'profit' (actually the whole difference between what you laid out and what you finally get, which may include reinvested income) is subject to complicated income tax assessment.

Personal tax on bond proceeds

Very roughly, this is to divide the profit by the number of years the bond has been held; then this sum (or 'slice') is added to your current year's income. If this total puts you into a higher income bracket, then you have to pay that particular rate of tax (but minus relief for basic rate, already paid by the fund). You pay at that rate on the 'slice', the amount of tax being multiplied by the number of years in the life of the bond.

If you have never come across the mechanics of bonds before you will now presumably be reeling with shock! However, it is necessary to form a view on your current and future tax position before venturing into bonds rather than straight investments. They are by necessity long term investments. They can have advantages to current high taxpayers who expect to be paying a lower rate when they are cashed (i.e. on retirement). There are rules allowing withdrawals every year of up to 5 per cent of the sum invested, and other features which can benefit the higher taxpayer, but advice is necessary on all such details.

There are many varieties of investment bond. Because they are insurance funds and not a straight unit trust, bond funds can be invested in other assets than stockmarket securities. The leading management groups offer a range of funds, some in general equities, some in overseas markets, some in gilts, some in fixed interest deposits, and (most prominently with some groups) in property.

'Switching' facilities: be wary

Most management groups offer low cost switching facilities so that you may transfer from say, an equity bond to a money deposit bond (if you think the market is too high) and then back again (when you think the time is right) at less cost than if you sold a unit trust to go into a bank deposit or building society, purchasing the trust again later. You may do this without incurring any intermediate liabilities. The range of investments within these switching facilities are now very wide, with most major overseas markets, gilts and property all available.

A word of warning on this, however. You may feel sure about the timing of your switches: if so, good luck with them. But untimely and too frequent switching can reduce your investment performance.

Property bonds
The ability to buy a piece of real estate, with all the traditional attractions of this genre, was one of the earliest and most powerful factors in the growth of bonds. However, a property bond is a rather different animal from an investment in a share portfolio. Buying new properties is a difficult and time consuming task. Buying good properties is becoming more difficult in the UK. Buying overseas carries its risks. The valuation of the property already in the portfolio is a matter of judgment by the valuers of the fund. It is not the same as the daily market value of shares. Therefore, the price of a property bond is only a rough guide, at any one time, to the value of its holdings, though it is the price at which the bond will be bought or realised. Property often comes in big blocks, and quick disposals are difficult. So property funds have to hold relatively large liquid funds (i.e. cash) on hand, to cover withdrawals by bondholders, as well as the need for quick finance in unexpected acquisitions. So you shouldn't expect the same performance from such a bond as from a single good property, or indeed (in the longer term) from a good equity fund.

27

Using charts and other investment systems

If you can correctly spot when any share or the whole stockmarket is going to change course, upwards or downwards, then you can make a lot of money. If you were possessed of this gift you wouldn't need to know very much about individual companies.

In search of this crock of gold, this key to fortune, investment enthusiasts over the years have devised many systems which have aimed at spotting trends in shares, or points of cheapness or dearness.

The most prominent of these systems is the use of share price charts to predict future movements. The use of charts starts from the assumption that a share price is the point at which buying pressure and selling pressure are equal. This is of course true in principle (even though a quoted price may in some smaller companies remain untested by any buying or selling for long periods). Changes in the balance of buying or selling create movements in this price. Some of these form trends and patterns, which are many times repeated over the cycles of individual shares and of stockmarkets, and can therefore suggest possible subsequent movements.

One of the most significant of these is the establishment of a bottom price level for a share: a sort of floor. Sellers have driven down the price. At some point the buyers give enough 'support' to stop the downward trend. The share may rise a little, then sink to its support level again. Let us say that the share fluctuates between 90p and 100p for some time, after a steady fall from 200p. Then, one day, the price breaks out from this 'channel' and rises to 110p or 115p. Clearly, the sellers at 100p have either all sold, or have changed their minds. Or the buyers have acquired more confidence. Or both.

In these circumstances, if the share had previously fallen without much interruption from 200p, there is some chance that the share will retrace a large part of its fall.

The chart of the share price of F. H. Lloyd, a steelmaking group which suffered badly from the decline in its market in the early eighties, is an interesting example of a big fall followed by a lengthy channel of dealings. The chart is drawn by the 'point and figure' method, whereby each change in the price is marked by a cross if it is upward, and a zero if it is downward. So it doesn't record time – only share movement. In this way, it highlights the buying and selling moods of the investors in the share. Now, at the point recorded, Lloyd shares showed no sign of diverging from the pattern you can see. It should be clear that an advance taking the price over 45p would be a very encouraging signal (and in fact, the share subsequently did just that and rose to 70p at one point fairly directly).

The reverse pattern may also be seen. After a continuous rise from, say, 20p, a share may meet 'resistance' at some level as a result of selling, and fluctuate around this level in a channel. If it suddenly drops below this channel, the implications of a much greater fall will be clear.

The 'point and figure' chart of the shares of Fidelity Radio shows this sort of heavy resistance at the top. In this case we can see the complete history of a rise through a previous lower 'base' (up to 80p) which promised well, and did indeed deliver that promise with an ascent to 177p. Then followed a series of moves which became more ominous as they developed. The fall through this 'top area' to 145p was a final danger signal, which proved very accurate in the event.

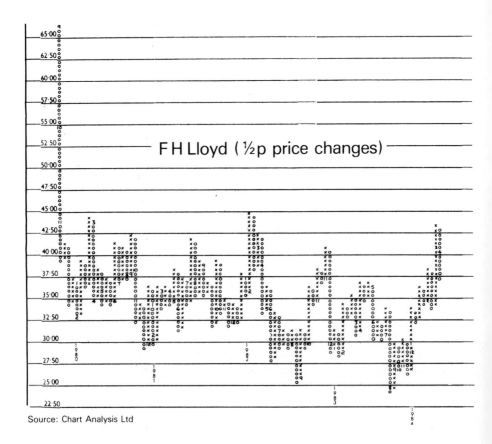

F H Lloyd (½p price changes)

Source: Chart Analysis Ltd

A lot depends on how long the floor of 'support' or the ceiling of 'resistance' continues. The longer such a precarious balance is held, the more likely it is that a breakout – in either direction – will be a signal for a bigger movement in that direction.

Patterns such as this are seldom clear-cut. Sometimes a share may make a 'double bottom' by zigzagging in a 'W' shape. A 'double top' is the reverse – an 'M' shape. Sometimes a sort of 'head and shoulders' can be discerned after a long rise, and a reverse head and shoulders after a long fall.

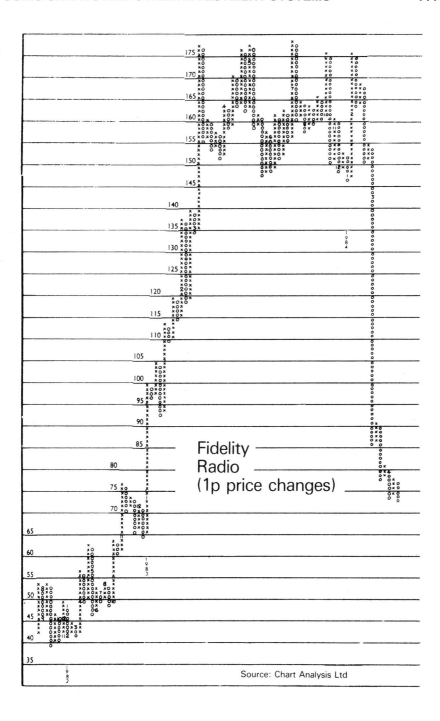

Fidelity
Radio
(1p price changes)

Source: Chart Analysis Ltd

In between, whilst a share is rising or falling, there may be intermittent patterns of temporary 'resistance' (on the way up) or 'support' (on the way down). Any of these may turn into points of change in trend. But if they don't do so, these patterns tend to assume the opposite function subsequently, if and when the share does change its trend at a lower level.

For example, suppose a support level is visible in a chart at 80p to 90p. This eventually gives way, and the share falls to around 50p then begins to climb again. That support level then becomes a resistance to the rise, because some of the buyers who got it wrong at 80p will be tempted to sell out when they see their original money again.

The permutations of chart reading are numerous and its exponents all have their variations on the themes. It is by no means proven as a method on its own. There is just as much uncertainty about most chart patterns as there is in any other systematic method of assessing shares and stockmarkets. However, the two basic concepts of resistance and support are useful as part of the whole process of selection and timing in investment. There are certainly some occasions when a share is revealed as suspect (dear) or promising (cheap) by looking at its chart.

THE HIGH YIELD PORTFOLIO SYSTEM

Another quite different approach to the problem of identifying cheap or dear stocks is the High Yield Portfolio system. The *Investors Chronicle* has run such a system regularly since 1956, issuing a new portfolio and reviewing progress every six months. The system is based on the assumption that the stockmarket tends to overdo its pessimism (as well as its optimism) about some shares from time to time; that the single most obvious measure of this is the yield on the share; and that although some of these high yielding shares will prove to be duds, in a portfolio of them the successes will adequately cover the risk. In one respect this will be a portfolio of 'recovery situations'. But the measure is specific, and mechanical. And since there has to be a yield, it is real enough.

Many unit trusts have been formed on roughly the same lines: the intention may be primarily to obtain the income but the result can also include capital performance. This is because when the yield on any share drops below your selected average, it has to be sold, and replaced with another share of the right minimum yield. If the yield has dropped because the share has risen more than the market, you have achieved capital performance, even if you also miss the rest of the rise in the share. If the yield has dropped because the dividend has been cut, well, at least the system obliges you to cut your loss without procrastinating. These two moves can be difficult to carry out without the disciplir ᴄ of the system.

POUND COST AVERAGING

Another useful system is that of Pound Cost Averaging. This is a fancy term for putting a specific constant sum of money into the market at regular intervals. It can be applied to the purchase of individual shares, but the disadvantage here is that you don't spread risk very easily, and small purchases are costly in dealing charges, so it is usually applied through unit trusts or a unit-linked life policy.

The principle involved is that your money buys more shares or units if the market falls and fewer if it rises. So you automatically increase your exposure at times when this might go against the grain. In highly volatile markets, with a longer term upward trend (as the UK has been for a long time) the arithmetic works in your favour. As with the High Yield system, the real point is that it overrules your natural human hesitancy – and mitigates the very human trait of doing the wrong thing at the wrong time!

28

Your broker and your shares

Your first practical steps in investment start when you make contact with your stockbroker. In an earlier chapter I mentioned some of the formal ways in which you can establish an introduction – through your bank manager or other professional contact, or through the agency of the Stock Exchange list of brokers who offer their services. However you reach this stage, the next step is to call on him personally if you can possibly do this. This will cut through a lot of potential misunderstandings. Give him a full picture of your circumstances and requirements. His advice will be the better for it.

Shares or unit trusts?
If you are a very small investor, he may conclude that you ought to start in unit trusts, not individual shares. You may not want to go along with this, or not entirely. If you do, make the most of his expertise in selecting the trusts. Some stockbrokers run their own 'in-house' unit trusts. Administration of Personal Equity Plans will be undertaken by many stockbrokers.

If you still think that you want to do your own thing, and if your broker takes you on in this capacity, he will be able to advise you on the first choices for your share portfolio, and to suggest subsequent sales and 'switches' from one stock to another. But he won't have the time to keep his eye on your shares continuously, so you must keep in touch with him. Don't overdo it though. Keep it for when you have a definite view or a real query.

Stockbroker services
Stockbrokers who deal mainly with private clients usually publish a regular newsletter which covers general opinion and specific share recommendations. Individual share decisions are still a matter between you and your broker personally. But such circulars will help to keep you in touch with the firm's thinking and may suggest courses of action, sometimes on technical points such as tax matters. Many stockbrokers nowadays specifically run advisory departments on taxation and other aspects of personal financial planning.

When buying or selling shares, I have referred to the need to get your ideas clear on price before you approach your broker. Specify any price limit you want him to observe, for the time that you want it. Decide in advance whether you would want to call it off if you can't get your price, or whether you would then be willing to do the deal 'at best' (i.e. at whatever price your broker can get). Your broker will help as much as he can, but there are several stages between him and a final bargain, so you must be aware of the scope for variation.

Your share deals do not normally have to be settled up immediately, as I have pointed out. (That is, except for gilt-edged deals, traded options and most foreign shares.) All deals are netted out during the Account for payment on Settlement Day.

Settlement of deals

Settlement, in the Stock Exchange, includes the collection of certificates for shares sold and arrangements for the transfer of ownership, which is finalised by the companies involved. The process has been eased by the introduction of a centralised computer-based pool for all stock, known as Talisman. However, the stockbroker is still responsible for the 'input' to the system.

This, in fact, includes all the documents relating to any holdings you may sell. As a buyer you only have to complete the contract note, pay before settlement day and then wait for your share certificate.

As a seller, you will also get a stock transfer form. You should fill this in as soon as possible and send it back to your broker along with the certificate or certificates involved.

Share certificates are your proof of ownership and you should obviously keep them safe, preferably in a good filing system. Or you may want to keep them at the bank (for a fee, of course) which you can arrange when you first start with your broker.

Promptness in sending off material to your broker will contribute your little bit to the smoother working of the system, and not least, will earn the goodwill of your broker – which can't be bad for your investment affairs.

Allocation of dividends and share issues

Where this really matters is when dividends, scrip issues, rights issues and other documentary receipts are attached to shares. When you buy a share, the company may be declaring a dividend or making an issue. The Stock Exchange establishes its own calendar for when these events affect the buyers or sellers of shares. There are certain Stock Exchange dates when a share is quoted 'ex dividend' or 'ex capitalisation' (scrip) or 'ex rights' or 'ex all' (when there has been more than one issue). The prefix 'ex' means that the share, so far as the Stock Market is concerned, no longer has the right to that dividend, etc. Before going 'ex' in the market, a share is sometimes described as being 'cum dividend' or scrip etc. But it is also assumed to be such if there is no prefix at all.

If you have sold a share 'cum div' you may still receive the dividend from the company because the register has not yet been changed. But this dividend belongs to the buyer, and should be sent on to your broker, as soon as possible. You will appreciate the usefulness of this when you are at the other end of the chain, and have not received a due dividend on shares you may have purchased 'cum div'. (In fact your broker will handle this for you, and you will get the dividend in due course.) Dividends straight from the company arrive as twin documents, one being the net payment (encashable) and the other being the voucher showing the amount of tax deducted at source which you will need for your own income tax computations. In the case of transferred dividends, your broker will supply you with proof of this tax deduction for the taxman.

29

Approaching the investment tax sums

It may sound paradoxical, but my first piece of advice on taxation as it affects your investment affairs is to forget it!

Forget it when you make your decisions that is. Your first criterion should be whether you or your advisors, whoever they may be, regard this or that investment as likely to make money for you or not.

To be more specific: don't buy an insurance-linked bond just because it offers some future tax advantage, as against a unit trust. Don't buy shares with low dividend yields just because you want to avoid income. Make your first decision on the basis of how attractive the offering seems to you purely as an investment proposition.

Obviously, the wealthier you are, the larger your estate, the more precedence will the tax angle take in all your decisions. And even the modestly-endowed professional person needs proper tax advice – particularly on capital transfer tax (which is not covered here) and how it relates to his total assets including his house. Pensions and pension arrangements also involve tax as a top priority.

What follows is a basic outline of the principles, though you will need more detailed advice as you get more involved in the game.

Income tax on investments

First, income tax. There are a few UK investments which pay income without any tax deductions at source (apart from bank and National Savings interest). These include British Government stocks bought on the National Savings Stock register (through the Post Office). However, all dividends from UK shares or unit trusts are taxed at source. What you get is the net dividend, after tax at Basic Rate (29 per cent) plus a voucher for the 'tax credit'.

UK company tax, since 1972, has been based on the principle of treating the company and the shareholder as linked together for taxation purposes. I have covered some of the details in earlier chapters. The company pays corporation tax currently at a rate of 35 per cent. Within this total percentage, all dividends to ordinary and preference shareholders have tax deducted by the company, at the current 29 per cent. Because this tax has already been paid, whereas you are not necessarily liable to personal tax, it is called a 'tax credit' in your tax return. If you don't pay tax, you can reclaim this tax already paid on your behalf. If you pay more than the basic rate, you will have to pay the balance later.

Bear in mind that the 'gross' taxable amount of the dividend is your net receipt plus the credit: for example if you receive £71 with a credit of £29 any higher rate of tax is calculated on the basis of the £100.

Higher rate tax

Investment income is added to your other sources of income for each year to establish your rate of tax. After your allowances are deducted, the 1986/87 tax on 'earned' income is 29 per cent on the first £17,200 then 40 per cent on the next £3,000 and higher rates thereafter. Before the Budget of March 1984 there was also an 'Investment Income Surcharge' of 15 per cent on all dividends and interest over a certain sum, but this is now abolished.

As I have noted, basic rate tax is already deducted from most dividends. But higher rate tax is not. For example, if your salary is (by chance!) exactly £17,200 after allowances, and you also received £1,000 in gross investment income (which could be £710 in net dividends and £290 in tax credits) then you have paid all your basic rate 'at source' (by PAYE and through the companies). But you are then liable to higher rate tax at 11 per cent on the extra £1,000 (i.e. the 40 per cent minus basic rate).

Your higher rate tax assessments are made (though sometimes delayed by strikes!) after the end of the tax year on that financial year's income.

The reductions in the top rates of income tax in recent years, and the abolition of investment income surcharge, have made the need to watch the level of investment income much less pressing. But on top of a salary, higher rate tax is going to bite. So obviously your choice is going to be influenced by this. By all means seek advice, and where you see a good investment without income (say the capital shares of a 'split' investment trust), this may be one answer. But beware of too complicated a contract framed merely to cut out the taxman.

CAPITAL GAINS TAX

Capital gains tax is the tax that, on principle, you shouldn't mind paying, because it implies success in your main aim as an investor. I should qualify this: on investments *dating from 1982 onwards* it will imply real success – because with the new rules of indexation, which started in 1982 and were revised in 1985, paying the tax will mean you have very adequately beaten inflation. Nonetheless, since CGT is levied at a rate of 30 per cent, you ought to know how to lessen its impact.

Exemptions from gains tax

Let us start by listing the main cases where you definitely won't be paying it, even when you have made gains exceeding inflation.

First, you don't have to pay it on net gains of up to £6,300 per annum. This exemption is the figure for the financial year 1986/87. The figure will be increased each financial year by the rate of increase of the Retail Price Index, measured over the previous calendar year.

For this purpose, the exemption figure applies to the net gains of a man and his wife together. Offsetting this disadvantage, transfers between husband and wife are not subject to gains tax.

Notice that I use the term 'net' gains when referring to the exemption. Realised losses are set against realised gains to establish a net figure in any one tax year. This must be done even if it brings the resultant net gains below the exemption limit. Suppose, for example that you had realised gains of £6,000 in 1982/83, and also losses of £2,000. You would have to use up the whole of the loss and show a net gain of £4,000, meaning part of the exemption would go to waste. On the other hand, if you realise net losses in any one year, these net losses may be carried forward. Suppose you had realised your gains of £6,000 in 1982/83 but also losses of £8,000. Your net loss of £2,000 on the year is carried forward and used in the following year to offset any gains realised in that year. You don't have to use up the whole of this £2,000, only as much as will reduce your gains to the exemption figure. For example, if you made gains of £6,300 in 1983/84, when the exemption figure was £5,300, then you would only need to use up £1,000 of the carried forward net losses, leaving another £1,000 to be set against future gains.

This is the most important exemption from the tax for the smaller investor. The other major exemption is that on gilt-edged and certain other fixed interest stocks. In the 1985 Finance Act, CGT was totally abolished on these stocks as from 1 July, 1986. So the 'profit' on redemption of gilt-edged holdings, even if it beats inflation, will not be taxed. Naturally, though, you don't get tax relief for gilt-edged losses.

The third type of exemption from CGT is indirect. It applies when you hold the shares of an investment trust or units in a unit trust. Although you may be personally liable for CGT when you sell the units or shares (depending on all the normal rules) you will not have to bear the cost of tax on the management of the unit or investment trust portfolio because trusts are exempted from CGT. Thus if you do realise a gain on a unit trust holding, and if you can use your exemptions, it will then not have been taxed at all.

There is also a fourth category of exemption, which embraces both CGT and income tax: the 'Personal Equity Plan', introduced in the 1986 Budget with effect from January 1987, which is referred to elsewhere.

How gains and losses are defined
What constitutes a gain or a loss for CGT purposes? It is the difference between your 'base cost' and the net sum which you realise on disposal. Your base cost will be the 'consideration' (i.e. the price paid for the shares) plus all the allowable expenses, which is in effect the total bill from your broker, covering commission, stamp duty etc. Your net realisation will be the same in reverse, the price you get for the shares minus the selling expenses.

Before 6 April 1982, the base cost remained the same, subject to amendments which I will deal with later. After 6 April 1982, the base cost is indexed to the Retail Price Index.

History of gains tax
Before going any further into the details of the current gains tax rules, a bit of historical background might be useful.

Capital gains tax was first imposed on 6 April 1965. Those who hold shares bought before that date have a series of choices as to what they wish to take as their 'base value' for capital gains tax purposes. I shall not detail them here, because they can involve complications which need the advice of a stockbroker. But put at its simplest, holdings dating from before 6 April 1965 can form a separate category for tax purposes. One of the choices was to take the 6 April 1965 date as the base date for the share value. This is popularly known as the 'Domesday' value.

The next radical change in the tax was introduced on 6 April 1982. Between 1965 and 1982 CGT for most normal share deals operated on a system whereby successive transactions in any one share were 'pooled' for tax purposes. Suppose you bought 100 XYZ shares at 200p giving a base cost of £200. Some time later you bought another 100 at 300p, an extra cost of £300. Your amended base cost then became £500 (£200 + £300) for 200 shares. If you later sold half your holding (i.e. 100 shares) for £400, your gain for tax purposes would be your proceeds of £400 set against the same proportion (i.e. a half) of your pooled cost of £500. The gain would be £400 − £250 = £150.

I will return to the mechanics of 'pooling' again later. This brief example is to show how the tax operated until 6 April 1982. On that date, the Government introduced a system of indexation, with an allowance based on the rise in the Retail Price Index over the period of holding. The rules were restrictive, however. There was no indexation allowance for the first year of a holding. There was no allowance for losses. So you could not set losses against gains. You could no longer 'pool' your individual holdings in any one share, because of these two restrictions.

The 1982 'frozen pool' and the 'new holding'

In the Budget of 1985, these restrictions were removed. So 'pooling' of holdings returned. One feature remains of the 1982 change. Indexation of holdings only begins from 6 April 1982. So any holdings from before that date have no full protection against the high inflation years of the 70s. However, there is *some* relief, because in the 1985 Budget along with the abolition of the restrictions referred to above, the Chancellor made another concession. You may now base the indexation allowance on the *6 April 1982 market value,* not as was previously the case on the *original cost.* Thus if you still have a holding of shares bought for 20p each in 1970, and if these had risen to 200p at 6 April 1982, your indexation allowance now starts at ten times the original level. So if you were to sell these shares at some date, after 20 per cent of inflation, your allowance would be 40p, and not 4p: quite a difference!

If you have followed me so far, you may now appreciate that the 6 April 1982 date is another sort of 'Domesday', like the 1965 one. Because there is no indexation before 1982, you can not 'pool' your holdings with current purchases. So individual holdings on 6 April 1982 now form a separate asset referred to by the inelegant title of the 'frozen pool'. If you have any holdings of this kind you should get a valuation as at this date from your stockbroker, to establish your base for the indexation allowance.

For potential investors who have not yet braved the stockmarkets or acquired any unit trusts, and for recent investors whose first purchases were made after 6 April 1982, the only rules to follow are the 'new pooling' rules.

For shareholders with holdings which date back before 1982, and especially those who also have holdings from before 1965, the tax permutations under the new regime may be complicated, although much less so than under the 1982 Act. Their main task when selling will be to 'identify' the shares sold with the right purchase. The 'order of identification' for sales after 5 April 1985 is as follows:

1. Purchases on the same day.
2. Purchases within one month before or after the sale (only affects companies, not individuals).

3. Purchases in the nine calendar days before disposal date (to stop anyone from getting one month's indexation allowance 'for free').
4. Purchases in the 'new holding' from 6 April 1982 (this is the first identification rule likely to affect most investors).
5. Purchases in the 'frozen pool' as at 5 April 1982 (the second important rule for investors). This pool will also contain shares from before 6 April 1965 for those who elected to take the 1965 date as their base cost.
6. Purchases before 6 April 1965 if no election for 1965 values was made.
7. Purchases after the disposal (aimed at those who have speculated in the 'Account' by 'selling short').

For most individual investors, the two main identification periods are No. 4 and No. 5, with No. 6 if you have held shares from the pre-1965 date without opting to have these valued on the original 'Domesday'. For example, suppose you have a holding of 2,000 ABC shares, of which you bought 500 in 1964, 500 in 1970 and 1,000 in 1984. If, in 1986, you sell half your holding (1,000 shares) these will be deemed to be those purchased in 1984: that is, the 'new holding'. To take the very simplest of calculations (I will deal with the pooling of 'new holdings' later), let us suppose that your 1984 purchase cost you £3,000, that you sold in 1986 for £4,000, and that interim inflation had been 10%. Your purchase cost would then be £3,300 (£3,000 plus £300 'indexation allowance'). Your gain for tax purposes would be £700.

If, instead of selling only 1,000 shares, you sold 1,500, then the arithmetic would be the same on the first 1,000, but the subsequent 500 shares (sold for £2,000) would have a different cost. Suppose your first purchase of 500 shares in 1964 had cost £100, and that you had opted for a 6 April 1965 value of £125. Your 1970 purchase of 500 shares cost, say, £150. So the 'pooled' cost of these 1,000 shares is £275. Now let us suppose that, on 6 April 1982 they were worth a magnificent £2,750. What would be your gain on the sale of 500 of these?

First of all, their cost (without indexation) is £275 for 1,000, so this becomes £137.50 for 500. If inflation were 25% between 6 April 1982 and the 1986 sale, then indexation would be £343.70 (remember that indexation is on the 1982 *value*). So the total cost would be just over £481. Matched with the sale proceeds of £2,000, the gain, therefore, is £1,519.

So your total gain on the sale of the 1,500 shares for £6,000 would be £2,219 (£700 on the 'new holding' of 1,000, and £1,519 on the 'frozen pool' holding).

Any further sales of your holding would be matched against the 'frozen pool'. But if you were to buy more ABC shares, then these would once more be the first to get matched with any subsequent sale. You could, in fact, continue to deal in ABC shares without having to involve your 'frozen pool', so long as you never sold more than your 'new holding'. Whether this would be advantageous or not depends on the rest of your overall gains tax position in any one period.

Bear in mind that the indexation of pre-1982 holdings will never be really adequate, so that establishing net gains from the 'frozen pool' which are within the annual exemption figure can be one way of guarding against future tax bills if inflation takes off again.

For those who take their profits on pre-1982 holdings and consolidate their investments into 'new holdings', and for those who only started to invest after 5 April 1982, the new pooling rules are the only ones to consider.

The 'new pooling' rules

The straightforward idea of pooling is that a holding of the same class of shares is treated as a single 'asset' which grows as more of the same shares are purchased and diminishes as part of the holding is disposed of. The new pooling rules have to incorporate indexation and this is done by updating the base cost of the pool (by adding the indexation allowance) just before any new transaction in the share. Suppose you buy 100 XYZ Company shares at 200p each, net of all expenses. Your base cost is £200. Later, you add to your holding by buying another 100, at 300p each, costing £300. Your pool is now £500 for 200 shares, without taking indexation into account.

Assume that the RPI has risen by 10 per cent over the period between these transactions. The Indexation Allowance will be 10 per cent of the original base cost of £200, i.e. £20. So the original cost of £200 becomes £220 and to this is added the new item of £300. Thus the indexed pool cost is now £520.

Now supposing that after a further interval, during which the RPI rises by another 10 per cent, you sell 100 XYZ shares at a price which gives you net proceeds of £350. The base cost of the whole pool (£520) needs to have the extra amount of indexation allowance added at this point, which is £520 × 10 per cent = £52. The indexed pool cost just prior to the sale is therefore £572.

You have, of course, only sold a proportion of the holding: a half in this case but since it would not always be a simple figure, take the Revenue's method and call it 100 ÷ 200 = 0.5. The proceeds are only 0.5 of the holding so the base cost has to be 'apportioned' in the same way, i.e. £572 × 0.5 = £286. Your gain for tax purposes is therefore £350 − £286 = £64. And the remaining pool of shares is £286.

The same principles apply to your pool of XYZ shares even if the transaction had resulted in losses. If by some mischance your shares had collapsed in price since the second purchase and your sale of 100 shares only realised £100, then the base cost being the same and the apportionment being the same, you would have a loss of £186 (i.e. £286 − £100).

READY RECKONER ON THE RETAIL PRICE INDEX

Jan 1974: 100	*Monthly figures (published on the following mid-months)*				
	1982	1983	1984	1985	1986
January		325.9	342.6	359.8	379.7
February		327.3	344.0	362.7	381.1
March	313.4	327.9	345.1	366.1	381.6
April	319.7	332.5	349.7	373.8	385.3
May	322.0	333.9	351.0	375.6	386.0
June	322.9	334.7	351.9	376.4	385.8
July	323.0	336.5	351.5	375.7	
August	323.1	338.0	354.8	376.7	
September	322.9	339.5	355.5	376.5	
October	324.5	340.7	357.7	377.1	
November	326.1	341.9	358.8	378.4	
December	325.5	342.8	358.8	378.9	

How do you keep up with the RPI? This figure is published in the middle of each month for the previous month. It is featured every month by the *Financial Times*, Post Offices display the current RPI as part of their routine announcements. The Inland Revenue periodically produces a table for each financial year, which it will supply on request. Your broker will also have a record and can give you an accurate measure. The table on page 121 shows the RPI figures from the Domesday of March 1982 to June 1986.

The Revenue's way of calculating an RPI increase is to use the formula:

$$\frac{RT - RI}{RI}$$

RT is the RPI at the date of the 'transaction' (i.e. a sale, or another purchase or any other transaction which needs an indexation allowance to be added) and RI is the 'identified' date (i.e. the last point where indexation allowance was added). For example, if you sold shares in January 1985 and the last previous transaction was in June 1982, the calculation would be, as you can see from the table:

$$(359.8 - 322.9) \div 322.9 = 0.114$$

It doesn't really matter how you calculate it as long as you recognise that this is an increase of 11.4 per cent. But the decimal figure is how the Revenue expresses the changes in its tables and it calls these the 'indexation factors'. You simply multiply your base cost by this 'factor' to obtain the allowance. Thus, if your cost were £500, the indexation allowance in this case would be £500 × 0.114 = £57.

Profits, gains and losses

Of course, you won't have to account to the Revenue for any transactions if your net gains in any one year are less than the exemption figure. This may be obvious. But if you want to avoid the tax permanently it will be useful, even when gains are below exemption level, to keep a check on your position every so often. Clearly, you are interested in your *money* gains or losses. You might just as well do occasional calculations on your potential *tax liability*.

Bed-and-breakfast

One important tactic in maintaining your net gains consistently below the exemption level is the 'bed-and-breakfast' transaction. This was made uneconomic by the first indexation rules but has regained its usefulness after the 1985 changes. 'Bed-and-breakfast' entails the sale of shares at the end of one dealing day and their repurchase first thing on the next. Since this involves very little risk of a change in the basic quotation price of the share, your broker can usually arrange this at low cost: one commission fee and a small 'turn' in the price. With unit trust units there may well be often a set fee which can be negligible on large transactions.

The first assumption in bed-and-breakfast transactions is that you do not want to part with the shares concerned: otherwise you might as well just sell them! Motives for bed-and-breakfast are: first, if you look as though you might finish the year with net gains over the exemptions limit, you can reduce this by realising losses in a 'b and b'; second, if you want to manage your gains tax liability over the longer term by realising some gains periodically in a stock you continue to hold.

Useful as this sort of deal can be, remember that it does have a cost, albeit lower than a conventional sale and repurchase. One rough rule of thumb is that the loss you are going to realise ought to be at least 10 per cent to make the saving of tax worthwhile. With 'flat fee' arrangements as with some unit trusts, you can compare this with the size of the bargain involved.

30

Share issues and gains tax

I have pointed out earlier in this book that a scrip issue in your shareholdings is merely a bookkeeping transaction. It leaves you with the same total value as you had before the issue, but with more shares at a correspondingly lower price.

The CGT implications follow from this. If you have a holding of 1,000 shares purchased at 200p, your original base cost is £2,000. If your company makes a one-for-two scrip issue, you will then have 1,500 shares. Your original base cost remains the same. The fact that it is spread over 1,500 shares, and is therefore 133.3p per share, makes no difference to the ultimate tax position if you sell any. The indexation allowance is the same in total. (However, you shouldn't forget that the original share purchase price needs an ex-scrip adjustment, for your own investment purposes!)

Rights issues, for tax purposes, are more complicated, because a new cash element is being introduced. However, it is merely another transaction for 'pooling' purposes and the rules remain the same. For example, suppose the issue in the example above had been a rights issue of one-for-two shares at 180p for each new share. If you subscribe to this, you emerge with 1,500 shares as with the scrip but you have had to put up cash of 500 × 180p or £900. So your new base cost is: the original £2,000 + indexation allowance on this + £900. If the RPI increase were 5 per cent (indexation factor 0.05) then your new base cost would be (£2,000 + £100) + £900 = £3,000 for 150 shares.

Selling your rights

Of course, you may not wish to subscribe to a proposed rights issue, either wholly or in part. You may then wish to sell your 'rights' to the new shares. As you may recall, the rights are first issued as 'allotment letters' which can be sold as 'nil paid' (i.e. without subscribing).

The principle for tax assessment (and also the basic investment situation) is that you are selling part of your holding. So you may be liable to gains tax if you have made a profit. Just how much of the holding is being sold is decided by the amount you realise from the sale of the nil-paid rights, versus the market value of the 'parent holding' of shares on the same day.

The formula is $A \div (A + B)$ where A is the realised amount from the sale of rights, and B is the market value of the parent holding (plus of course any rights you haven't sold).

In our example above, if the original 1,000 shares were quoted in the market at 220p when you sold your rights, and if you sold all your rights (i.e. 500) at 40p each, then the apportionment would be: £200 (i.e. 500 rights at 40p) ÷ (£200 + £2,200). This is one twelfth of the holding, or 8.3 per cent.

You then have to relate this back to your base cost immediately before the transaction to work out what slice of your pool has been sold. The base cost was £2,100 after indexation, so you have sold £2,100 × 0.83, or £174, of your pool, leaving it at £1,926 for future matching of transactions. So you have realised £200 with an apportioned cost of £174; a gain of £26.

Of course, nobody in their right mind would bother with all this for the small sums illustrated here. And you can avoid it altogether if you are likely to be well within the exemption limit. Moreover, where the cash received is less than 5 per cent of the market value of the total holding, there is an automatic exemption from immediate tax liability. In these cases the receipt is deducted from the original base cost for future gains tax purposes. This 5 per cent exemption applies not only to rights issues proceeds but to other forms of capital realised, such as small capital repayments by companies. So the arithmetic above is mainly to show you how the whole thing works, in all its glory! And to prepare you, of course, in case you do find yourself with a magnificent profit on any holding.

TAKEOVERS AND GAINS TAX

If a takeover bid for your shares does provide you with a magnificent profit, it can take two main forms. If you accept a cash bid, then it counts as a disposal for tax purposes. A bid wholly in shares does not. You simply transfer the base cost of your original holding to the new shares received, apportioning this amongst the shares in question. If you have a holding of 400 shares in XYZ bought at 100p (an original cost of £400) and you accept a two-for-one share exchange bid by ABC Company, you still have an original cost of £400 but you now have 800 shares so the cost has become 50p per share. Indexation is uninterrupted by the exchange.

If the bid is wholly in cash the calculation is exactly as though you had sold the shares in the market.

If the bid is part cash and part shares, then the base cost is apportioned between the two elements. In tax terms, it is a partial disposal.

Apportioning a split in a holding
Apportionment of any asset is decided by the relative market values of the separate parts at the time when the split occurs. In practice, the apportionment in a mixed bid is decided by the value of the share element on the first day of dealings in the new stock. For example, if the bid were of one ABC share plus 150p in cash for each XYZ share, then your total holding would be £600 in cash plus £600 in shares (400 ABC × 150p). The formula is described as A over A + B, where A is the £600 cash and B is the £600 market value of the new shares. In this case, you would be deemed to have sold 50 per cent of your holding.

Where a question of share valuation is concerned, the Stock Exchange has its own recognised procedures and you will be able to obtain the official share valuation from your broker, plus the official apportionment for tax purposes.

Since the ratio in the case above is 50/50, your base cost of £400 is apportioned in this way. Thus it now becomes £200 for the shares you still retain and £200 for the cash element. Your tax liability is £600 (the cash proceeds) minus £200 (base cost) plus indexation of this to the date of the bid.

Bids in two types of security

The principle of apportionment applies if the takeover terms offer two different classes of capital for your original shares, such as ordinary shares and convertible loan stock. The split is still decided by the ratio of the market prices for the two classes of capital on the first day of dealings. Of course, there is no immediate tax liability if you keep your new holdings. But the base cost is divided in the same way and thereafter each of the two holdings relates back to its own bit of the base cost. The indexation will also apply from the same base date for each holding.

GAINS TAX ON WARRANTS AND TRADED OPTIONS

These are taxed as though they were shares, as far as individual investors are concerned. If you simply buy and sell warrants and traded options, tax is on the gains from the transactions. Losses can be utilised in the normal way. If a traded option lapses (i.e. if it becomes unprofitable to subscribe for the underlying shares) then it also counts as a loss. The rules of the *writing* of options (i.e. selling options to others) work in reverse. Your fee for writing the option is a taxable profit if the option lapses. If it is 'exercised' and you have to sell the underlying shares, the whole operation is lumped together to establish a total figure of costs and receipts, resulting in a gain or loss as the case may be.

SUMMING UP

Let me repeat my first advice about tax: don't let it interfere too much with your decisions on investment grounds. Don't let it prevent you taking a profit when it seems otherwise sensible to do so. If you have recorded your transactions properly, with notes of the RPI included, you should be able to do the calculations later with the application of a few cold towels. Matching the right purchases with your disposals will be one of the complications. So will rights issues, if you get more than one in any holding. Ask your broker for his advice on the tricky questions, but have the facts at hand to enable him to help. Bear in mind the possibilities of Personal Equity Plans and the portfolio exemptions of unit and investment trusts from CGT. Naturally you should use the annual exemption as fully as is sensible. Where it appears economical, consider the use of 'bed-and-breakfast' transactions. With this armoury, together with indexation of gains and of the exemption limit, it should be possible for most smaller investors to forget about gains tax.

31

Where to get information and advice

If you have read this far, then I can assume that you are at least a prospective investor and I would hope you have some basic background to start you off, should your intentions turn into action.

This first thing you will need, as I have stressed throughout, is a clear idea of your aims. Are you after income or capital growth, do you want steadier shares or more speculative investments, and so on? The second thing you need at your own disposal is a system of records. I have emphasised this when discussing tax. But your choice of investment and your timing of buying and selling will be improved by knowing exactly what you have already done and where you stand at any moment. (It is surprising how many established investors don't!)

For capital gains tax purposes you will need to keep two price records for each share: one showing what you actually paid for it and the second showing how this base value will be up-rated monthly in line with the retail price index as a basis for calculating gains that are liable to tax.

Background on unit trusts
If you are going to concentrate mainly on unit trusts rather than shares, you will of course be saved some of the detailed decisions, because you can then buy 'ready made' policies (i.e. the pursuit of high yield or recovery or mainstream investments, etc.) as well as the portfolios which reflect them. But you still have to decide what the mixture should be and the 'cheapness' or 'dearness' of the trust's units at any one time.

Guidance in this, after you have defined your criteria, may well be provided by your stockbroker. But you should invest in some background first. The best single source of general information on UK unit trusts is the *Unit Trust Yearbook*. For the current situation in the trust world with records of performance and periodic reviews, you should get a copy of one of the monthly journals, *Money Management* or *Planned Savings*. These are designed for investment advisors rather than investors but are nevertheless valuable sources of information for the individual, too.

Background on companies
Background statistical information on shares is not assembled so specifically. Institutions in the City have access to plentiful statistical information, such as that provided by **Datastream** and by the **Exchange Telegraph** service on

companies, as well as the routine information provided by stockbrokers. This is either not easily available to the individual, or is likely to be too expensive, though most services will provide 'one-off' information on a single company – and your broker may be prepared to help. The *Hambro Company Guide* is a useful compendium of facts and figures on most UK companies. It is issued quarterly.

The most comprehensive practical way to acquire the statistics is to file your copies of the *Investors Chronicle* and use the quarterly index to locate each company as necessary, together with the periodic reviews of company sectors as further background. The monthly price information service in the *Investors Chronicle* gives performance information on the main companies and breaks them down by market sector.

When it comes to the point of action, to decisions on this or that share, or on the direction of the stockmarket, the sources are wider and more diffuse. As with the statistical background , you are not likely to have access to the 'high-powered' research comment provided for the City institutions. But your stockbroking firm is quite likely to issue a newsletter for private clients which will provide market background information: many of these are worthwhile reading. You can of course always ask your broker for specific information.

Read the Financial Press

In the end, when it comes to companies, the only really important source you lack is the personal contact with the companies themselves which the institutions have access to. There is nothing much you can do about this. But in every other way, your access to press comment and published information is as unrestricted as that of any professional investment group. The *Financial Times* will cover most market and company events as they occur. The *Investors Chronicle* will summarise and comment on these and analyse them to provide more facts and figures to go on. There will also be specific investment recommendations each week. The City pages of the Sunday press will feature various investigative themes and offer ideas on shares.

Market newsletters

There are also a number of specialised market newsletters, 'tip sheets,' which cater for idea-seekers. These include the old-established market mid-week *IC Newsletter*. Naturally enough, these publications are also scanned by the market professionals. A really good 'tip' from one of these letters (as indeed from the daily or Sunday press) can push up the price of the shares concerned in the short term, sometimes artificially. So beware: if you do decide to follow advice from these, or any similar publicised source, wait before you act.

'Inside' information – beware!

As an aside on this, I would advise you never to buy or sell a share on what purports to be 'inside' information from friends or acquaintances. Such sources are seldom what they seem, even in the privileged climate of the City. For every one that proves right there are many which prove unprofitable, some disastrous.

Rely more on your own judgment, after you have done your homework on the background facts and figures. 'Ideas' can be gained from general observation rather than specific share 'tips'. The *Investors Chronicle* publishes occasional analyses of shares in conjunction with Datastream, using the enormous statistical database of the latter to give lists of shares on criteria of net asset value, degree of liquidity, potential for recovery and so on. This is 'ideas' material which can prompt your own investigations.

All this advice, I know, is easier to give than to follow. You will in any case have to test it with your own experience – the only real teacher in the end. However, as with driving a car, there are better and worse ways of getting to your destination. I wish you every good fortune in your journey!

Publications:

The Unit Trust Yearbook. Published by Financial Times Business Information, 102 Clerkenwell Road, London EC1M 5SA.

The Hambro Company Guide. Published quarterly by Hemington Scott Publishing Ltd, Greenhill House, 90 Cowcross Street, London EC1M 6BH. £39.50 per annum.

Money Management. Published by Financial Times Business Information, Greystoke Place, Fetter Lane, London EC4A 1ND. £2.50 per copy.

Planned Savings. Published by United Trade Press, UTP House, 33-35 Bowling Green Lane, London EC1R 0DA. £3.50 per copy.

Information about The Stock Exchange, and about member firms, can be obtained from:

> The Information and Press Department, The Stock Exchange, London EC2N 1HP

or from the regional centres as follows:

> Northern Bank House, 10 High Street, Belfast BT1 2BP
>
> Margaret Street, Birmingham B3 3JL
>
> 28 Anglesea Street, Dublin 2
>
> Stock Exchange House, PO Box 141, 69 St Georges Places, Glasgow G2 1BU
>
> Silk House Court, Titheburn Street, Liverpool L2 2LT
>
> 6 Norfolk Street, Manchester M2 1DS

Glossary

Glossary of investment terms

'A' SHARES: See Non-Voting Shares.

ACCOUNT: The Stock Exchange Account is usually of two weeks duration, but some are of three weeks to even up the calendar. Most UK registered securities are 'settled for the Account', i.e. not for 'cash' or immediate payment. The Account system is to be altered under the new Stock Exchange procedures.

ACCOUNT DAY: See Settlement Day.

ADVANCE CORPORATION TAX: Usually known as ACT, this is the tax paid by companies on their dividends to shareholders. It is levied at the basic rate of income tax and in the hands of the shareholder it represents the 'tax credit' on the dividend.

ALLOTMENT LETTER: An official document from a company or its representatives stating that the holder has been allotted a specific number of shares or stock in an issue of some kind. Dealings in these used to be free of stamp duty, but are no longer so.

ASSENTED SHARES OR STOCK: Shares are quoted in this form where holders have indicated their acceptance of a bid or other capital arrangement. Any purchaser of such shares is then committed to acceptance.

ASSET VALUE: See Net Asset Value.

AUTHORISED CAPITAL: The nominal capital of a company which is authorised by its articles of association. It need not all be issued, but no issue can be made which exceeds the authorised sum.

AUTHORISED DEPOSITARY: An agent such as a bank, stockbroker or solicitor, who is authorised by the Bank of England to hold foreign and bearer stocks on behalf of their owners.

AVERAGING: Buying more of the same shares on a fall, or selling on a rise, in the hope of gaining advantage by the fluctuations. How useful this is depends on the circumstances.

●

BARGAIN: A purchase or sale on the Stock Exchange.

BEAR: Technically, a person who sells stock he does not hold in the hope of buying it back at a lower price. Used loosely to describe someone who thinks a price or prices will fall. By extension, a bear market is one where prices are under the primary influence of sellers.

BEARER STOCKS: Stocks whose ownership is not recorded centrally (see Registered Stocks) and which must be physically passed from seller to buyer to establish ownership.

BED AND BREAKFAST: Selling stocks and buying them back overnight so as to establish a profit or loss for capital gains tax purposes.

BENEFICIAL OWNER: The true owner of a share, as opposed to any name in which it may be legally held. (See Nominee.)

BID: To indicate the price at which one is prepared to buy shares. The bid price in a share quotation is the lower price, because it is the market maker's buying price. When a price is just quoted as 'bid', it implies that there are few sellers.

BIG BANG: The change in the rules of the Stock Exchange which occurred on 27 October 1986. So called because the abolition of fixed commission charges precipitated a complete alteration in the structure of the market.

BLUE CHIP: Originally an American expression, to denote the shares of companies which are well established, usually large, and highly regarded.

BONDS: Securities issued by governments or companies as debt. They are usually of fixed interest, are in bearer form, and have detachable 'coupons' for the claiming of interest. The term is also used for certain insurance-based investment funds.

BRITISH FUNDS: The official term for UK government stock (i.e. gilt-edged).

BULL: Originally, someone who buys shares in the hope he will be able to sell them at a higher price before having to pay for the purchase. Now, more usually, a person who thinks a price will rise. By extension, a bull market is one which is primarily influenced by buyers.

●

CALL: The amount of money which still has to be paid on any partly-paid issue. More than one call may be specified in certain issues.

CALL OPTION: The right to buy shares at an agreed price within a set period.

CAPITALISATION ISSUE: See Scrip Issue.

CASH FLOW: The amount by which a company's net resources are increased over the year. Investment analysts normally use this term as a shorthand for profit retentions plus depreciation. That is what the company's *trading* contributes to its resources (as opposed to sales of assets or issues of new capital).

CASH SETTLEMENT: Deals which are due to be paid for immediately, as distinct from those for the Account. Gilt-edged and new issue transactions are normally for cash settlement.

CERTIFICATE: The document signifying ownership of stock or shares. The certificate is transferred to the new owner or owners upon a sale of the shares. (See Transfer Deed.)

CERTIFICATION: The marking on the transfer deed, upon the sale of shares, to show that the certificate has been lodged with the company's registrars or with the Stock Exchange. This is necessary when the seller is not parting with all his holding, or when the shares are bought by more than one person. New certificates are then issued to cover the exact redistribution of ownership.

'CLOSING': Buying or selling to close a bargain opened in the same Account.

COMMON STOCKS: The North American term for ordinary shares or 'equities'.

CONSIDERATION: The cost of a purchase or the amount of a sale before brokers' commissions, charges, stamp duty and other transfer expenses. It is thus not the full cost for capital gains tax purposes.

CONSOLIDATED ACCOUNTS: The accounts of a company together with all its subsidiary companies, presented in one set of figures.

CONTANGO: Carrying over the settlement of a transaction from one Account to the next, for an extra consideration.

CONTINUATION DAY: The first day of a Stock Exchange Account.

COUPON: A warrant, detachable from a bond or share certificate, which must be presented for payment of interest or dividend to the appointed agents of the issuing authority or company.

CUM: The Latin prefix meaning 'with'. A share quoted 'cum dividend' carries the right to a recently declared dividend. 'Cum scrip' and 'cum rights' carry similar implications. The entitlement is normally there without the prefix being used.

CUMULATIVE: Usually used in connection with preference shares, where the share carries the right to receive arrears of dividend before any other dividends are paid on lower ranking stocks (such as ordinary shares).

CURRENT ASSETS: Those of a company's assets which are part of the regular turnover of the company: cash; bank deposit; marketable securities; debtors (i.e. money owed to the company for goods); and stock and work in progress.

CURRENT LIABILITIES: Those items which a company owes to others as part of its regular business: i.e. creditors (money owed to others for goods, materials or services); bank overdrafts or short-term loans; current tax bills; and dividends already declared but not yet paid.

CURRENT COST ACCOUNTING: The term used for the conversion of a company's accounting figures to show what the effects of inflation have been in any one annual period. A series of rules have been devised by the official accountancy bodies to try to show how inflation over the year has affected:

    (a) Fixed assets, including extra depreciation needed
        to cover replacement at higher cost.
    (b) The cost of replacing stock at higher prices.
    (c) The balance of money owed, and money owing,
        for goods and services.

CURRENT YIELD: The annual return, before tax, on an investment at the current price of a security, represented by the interest or dividend. In the case of gilt-edged stocks or other fixed interest stocks repayable at a specific date, it is known also as the flat yield. In this case it represents the annual return on the interest only; not on any increase in price on the maturity of the stock.

●

'DEALING FOR NEW TIME': The purchase or sale of shares in one Account, but for the next Account. This is permitted during the last two days of the old Account. It must be specified, and there may be a slightly different price quoted.

'DEALING FOR THE ACCOUNT': The purchase and sale (or the sale and purchase) of the same shares within the same Account. Commission is only charged on the 'opening' transaction.

DEBENTURE: A bond issued by a company, usually secured on its assets either specifically or in general. Debenture stock, as with gilt-edged, is quoted in units of £100 on the Stock Exchange.

DELIVERY: In the Stock Exchange, the formal transfer of the share certificate to the new owner.

DISCOUNT: A deduction made in the market price of a security for some reason. Government stocks may be issued at a discount to their maturity value, so as to create an element of capital gain as an attraction. Short-term Treasury bills are issued at a discount from their maturity value to create the equivalent of interest income. Shares may be priced by investors at a discount to their theoretical net asset value. Investment trust shares are often judged by the extent of the discount on their portfolio asset value. (See also Premium.)

DISCOUNTED: Events in the progress of a company or wider events in the economy are sometimes said to be 'discounted in the market': that is, they are allowed for in the stock or share prices concerned.

DIVIDEND: The distribution to shareholders out of company profit. UK dividends are declared net of tax (see Advance Corporation Tax) but with a tax credit to the holder. Nowadays, the dividend per share is expressed in pence, but may also be given as a percentage of the par value of the share.

DIVIDEND COVER: The number of times the net dividend is covered by the net earnings attributable to equity holders.

DIVIDEND WARRANT: The cheque for the dividend payment. This is accompanied by the voucher recording the amount of net dividend and the amount of tax credit (for the satisfaction of the Inland Revenue).

'DOLLAR PREMIUM': No longer a feature of investment since Exchange Control was lifted in 1979. It represented the extra price paid for foreign currency, above the commercial exchange rate, for the purchase of foreign investments.

'DUAL CAPACITY': Under the Stock Exchange rules as changed on 27 October 1986, the right of a firm to make markets in shares as well as to act as agents (brokers) in dealings with investors.

●

EARNINGS: Usually short for 'Earnings for Ordinary'. It is the net profit after tax, after any minority interest and after any preference dividends: that is, the profit available for equity holders. It is normally expressed as earnings per share to give a comparison with the dividend.

EARNINGS YIELD: Another way of comparing earnings with dividend, in addition to the use of 'times covered'. Calculated like the dividend yield, but using the maximum distributable amount per share. It is also obtained by multiplying the dividend yield by the dividend cover, if already known: i.e. a dividend yield of 5 per cent, with a dividend covered twice, would represent an earnings yield of 10 per cent.

EQUITY: That which is left over on property after all prior claims have been met. Thus, equity shares are entitled to the earnings and the assets of a company after all charges on prior capital.

EX: From the Latin meaning 'without'. A security whose price is quoted 'ex div' is transferred without the recently declared dividend. Likewise, 'ex scrip' or 'ex rights' means that any new buyer will not be entitled to a recent scrip issue or rights issue. Share prices quoted 'ex' are of course adjusted to reflect the absence of the rights concerned.

●

FIXED ASSETS: Assets, such as premises, plant and equipment, which are used as the basis for generating business, as opposed to current assets which are used in the course of business.

FLAT YIELD: See Current Yield.

FLOTATION: The issue on the Stock Exchange of stock in a new company.

FRANKED INVESTMENT INCOME: Dividends received by one company from another company which has already borne corporation tax on its profits. Dividend income of this sort is received from UK companies net of tax. It can thus be passed on by investment trusts and unit trusts without any extra taxation. The opposite, unfranked income, is that which as come from companies outside the UK, or from a non-company source (e.g. gilt-edged interest). Corporation tax has to be paid on this by the companies receiving it.

FULLY PAID: Shares where all the nominal capital is paid up. (See Partly-Paid.)

FUTURES: Contracts for the delivery or purchase of assets at a future date. These may be commodities of various kinds, or indeed financial assets such as bills and bonds. There is a futures contract in the FTSE 100 Index.

●

GEARING: This is the term normally used for the ratio of all the company's borrowings to its share capital. It is expressed as a percentage. In the total of borrowings, both fixed capital (debentures etc.) and net bank borrowings are included.

GILT-EDGED: The familiar name for UK Government stocks.

GOODWILL: The theoretical value to a company of its business connections. Together with such items as patents, royalties, trade markets, it forms what are known as 'Intangible Assets'.

GROSS: In the investment field, this means before deduction of income tax.

'GROSSING UP': The conversion of a net figure into a gross figure. In the case of net dividends from UK companies, it means adding back the 'tax credit'. This is necessary for yield calculations. All income tax assessments are based on gross income, and since investors' tax rates differ, yield comparisons must be on the gross figure.

'GROWTH STOCKS': Shares of companies where the earnings for shareholders are expected to grow significantly faster than average. The dividend yield on such shares will be lower than average since the overall return from future dividend increases and capital appreciation is expected to make up for this. You must expect such shares to respond more sharply than others to changed estimates of future growth – for better or for worse.

●

HISTORIC COST ACCOUNTS: The traditional method of accounting for profits and other balance sheet figures, making no allowance for inflation as in Current Cost Accounting. Thus, stock is valued at its original cost, not its current replacement cost. Fixed assets are entered at original cost, minus a depreciation figure based on that cost.

●

INDEX: There are three widely used general share indices of the London Stockmarket. The best known is the Financial Times Industrial Ordinary Index. This consists of thirty leading industrial shares. It is a simple index to calculate and is now produced hourly to give a measure of the movement of shares through each day. However, it is not an accurate measure of long-term market performance. The Financial Times Actuaries All Share Index has been used for this purpose since its compilation in 1962. This index is constructed more like the valuation of a portfolio. It contains 750 shares. It is also split into sub-indices measuring different sectors within the overall total. As well as the equity indices there are also other FTA indices covering gilts and other fixed interest stocks. The third index is the FTSE 100 Index, which contains 100 leading stocks and is calculated virtually continuously throughout each day.

INDEX-LINKED GILTS: A type of Government stock introduced to the general public in 1982. The stocks cover a range of maturities. Each has a very low 'coupon', but this payment is guaranteed to rise in line with the Retail Price Index. There is also a guarantee that the final redemption price will be linked to the RPI. There is, however, no minimum floor for the redemption price.

INFLATION ADJUSTED ACCOUNTS: See Current Cost Accounting.

INTRODUCTION: An issue of shares, not through an 'offer for sale', but through the 'market' (i.e. through stockbrokers and jobbers) such that there are shares available for the public to buy. This is the favoured method for the launching of an already established foreign company on the London market.

INVESTMENT TRUST: A company whose business is in the management of securities on behalf of its shareholders. It is granted various concessions (including freedom from gains tax on its portfolio) in return for which it must conform to certain limitations, including the obligation to distribute a large part of its investment income.

ISSUED CAPITAL: The capital which is actually held by shareholders, as distinct from authorised capital which is, as it were, held in reserve.

ISSUING HOUSE: The agency which co-ordinates all the arrangements for an issue of stock or shares. It is very often a merchant bank, but stockbroking firms also arrange issues.

●

JOBBERS: The original name for dealers in securities on the Stock Exchange. They had no direct contact with the public, the deals being done between them and stockbrokers. Under the new Stock Exchange System, there are firms which can act as dealers ('market makers') and also as brokers. This is called 'dual capacity'.

●

LIMIT: A restriction on the price at which a broker may buy or sell securities, set by the client.

LIQUID ASSETS: Cash or assets easily convertible into cash, such as marketable securities.

'LISTS CLOSED': Offers for sale have a limited period during which applications are considered. In effect, all serious applications will be in before the 'lists open'. Thus, the lists will normally close one minute later for fully subscribed issues.

LONG: A holder of shares with a bullish view. (See Short.)

LONGS: Long-dated Government stock (i.e. with redemption dates of over 15 years).

●

MARGIN: Speculators in some overseas stock markets (though not on the London Stock Exchange) are allowed to buy shares 'on margin'. This means that their stockbroker may lend them up to a certain proportion of the share's market price, with the share as collateral. The difference between the loan value and the market value is the 'margin', which they are required to pay: and also to preserve by paying up more, if the market price of the share falls.

MARKET MAKER: The term used under the Stock Exchange rules after October 1986 for the function formerly known as 'jobber'. The difference is that jobbing firms were clearly defined as separate from broking. Now, if they wish, firms may make prices in shares and also directly with investors in them.

'MEDIUMS': Medium-dated gilt-edged stock (i.e. with a life of between 5 years and 15 years).

MIDDLE PRICE: The half way point between the offer and bid prices on any single quotation. Share prices in newspapers are normally the middle price: and thus, if the quotation is a wide one, the implied dealing price will differ significantly.

MINORITY INTEREST: Those shareholdings in the subsidiary companies of a group which are held 'outside', in other words not held by the parent company. Earnings and assets due to these outside holders are recorded in the consolidated profit and loss account and the balance sheet. The term 'minorities' is also used where one or more large shareholders may control a company, leaving a smaller number in a 'minority position'. The term may be used where there is some conflict of interest between the two sets of holders.

●

NET ASSET VALUE: The net assets of a company for equity shareholders are the total assets of the company, minus all the liabilities in the balance sheet, minus all the prior capital (including debentures, loan stocks and preference shares). The 'N.A.V.' is this sum divided by the number of shares, to give a figure per share.

NET PROFIT: The profit of a company after depreciation, interest and tax. If there are preference dividends and minority interests, these must then be deducted to reach the profit attributable to equity shareholders.

NEW SHARES: Shares which have been issued but are still being dealt in 'free of stamp and fee' before they have been registered. They will have a slightly higher market price than 'old' shares because of this.

NOMINAL VALUE: (or par value) The face value of a share as against its market value. Par values may be of any amount, but 25p is now becoming the most common apart from the traditional £1. They have no real investment significance, being purely a matter of law and bookkeeping.

NOMINEE: This usually refers to a legal entity which holds shares on behalf of others. It is a normal practice where investments are being managed by a professional for a client (e.g by a unit trust). It can be a method of concealing the beneficial owner if he does not wish his identity to be obvious.

NON-VOTING SHARES: There are still a number of well-known companies whose voting equity capital is small and tightly controlled by directors or founding families, and whose main equity is in non-voting shares. These are often called 'A' shares. Holders of such shares will find themselves at a disadvantage in takeovers or in cases of controversy about company policy.

NO PAR VALUE: This is the normal type of share in North America. Ther is no par or nominal value, the share capital being defined merely by the number of shares.

●

OFFERED PRICE: The higher of the two prices in a quotation, being the price at which the market maker will sell to the broker.

'OFFERED NOT BID': A price at which there are potential sellers but no buyers.

OFFICIAL LIST: The Stock Exchange Daily Official List is the record of quotations, and bargains, for all listed securities. It gives details and dates of any dividends, rights or other pertinent information. This list is the arbiter for share valuations.

OFFSHORE: A term used for a fund which operates from a base in one of the 'tax-havens' outside the UK (such as Luxembourg, or the Cayman Islands) to obtain freedom from UK tax. Orginally, freedom from exchange control was also the aim, but this is currently not relevant.

OPTION: The right, on payment of option money, to buy a given security for a given price within a given period (call option), or to sell (put option), or the right both to buy or to sell (double option). (See also Traded Option.)

ORDINARY SHARES: Shares entitled to a company's earnings and its assets after all prior charges and claims have been met. (See Equity.)

●

PAR VALUE: See Nominal Value.

PARI PASSU: 'Equal in its position': a term used when an issue of stock or shares is made which has the same status as existing capital.

PARTLY-PAID: Shares whose full nominal value has not been paid up and where there is therefore a 'call' or 'calls' due on the balance. Very few UK companies nowadays use this type of share as their primary method of raising capital. Government stocks are sometimes issued in this way, with one or more calls at specified dates. The term is also used for the allotment letters in a rights issue before the cash is subscribed.

PLACING: An issue of stock or shares to a specific group of buyers. See Vendor Placing.

PORTFOLIO: A number of different securities held by one investor, either an individual or a body of some kind.

PREFERENCE SHARES: Shares with a fixed dividend, and with prior claims to both dividends and capital repayment over ordinary shares. They may be 'cumulative' (see separate entry). Preference shares have no priority over debentures, loan stocks and company creditors.

PREMIUM: The opposite of a discount (see separate entry). Most often used when the price of a security stands at more than some stated value, such as the paid-up value of a newly issued share or the net asset value of an investment trust.

PRICE EARNINGS RATIO: (PE): The number of times that a company's latest earnings per share goes into the current market price of that share. Sometimes referred to as the earnings multiple. The PEs on the back page of the *Financial Times* are calculated on earnings after the actual tax paid by the company. Many investment analysts do their own calculations of what the tax would have been without certain items of tax relief. They call the resulting multiple the 'fully taxed PE'.

PRIOR CHARGES: Debentures and loan stocks, whose interest is payable ahead of any dividends on share capital. This interest is an offset against corporation tax. Sometimes the term is also used to take in preference shares.

PRIORITY PERCENTAGES: This is one expression of the 'gearing' of a company's profits. The basis of the calculation is the company's net profit plus the net amount taken up by interest. Then, in order of priority, the cost of interest and dividend payments is compared with this sum. For example, debenture interest might take from 0 to 5 per cent of the profit: other interest might take from 5 per cent to 20 per cent; preference dividends might take from 20 per cent to 22 per cent; and ordinary dividends might take from 22 per cent to 50 per cent. This puts into perspective the amount of leeway in the profit figure for the servicing of all the company's obligations, and adds a new dimension to the 'cover' for dividends.

PROXY: A person empowered to act for another at a company meeting when voting takes place. Proxy forms are sent to shareholders and they may choose whether to give the company's directors the discretion to vote with this document.

PUT OPTION: The right to sell a specific share at an agreed price by a specific date.

●

QUICK ASSETS: See Liquid Assets.

QUOTATION: The price made in securities by market makers. The word quotation also implies Stock Exchange approval, since a quotation is 'granted' on new shares after this approval has been gained.

●

REDEMPTION DATE: The repayment date or dates for gilts, debentures and other stocks of this kind.

REDEMPTION YIELD: The flat yield on a stock (see entry) augmented by a percentage calculated as the annual equivalent of the final capital 'profit' on redemption. This is if the present purchase price is below the redemption price. If the present purchase price is *above* the redemption price, there will be a similar calculation, but negative: the flat yield will be diminished by it.

REGISTERED STOCKS: The normal type of share in the UK, where the ownership is recorded in the company's register. Their ownership changes by Deed of Transfer, after which registers are altered and new certificates made out. Bearer stocks (see entry) are transferred physically.

REGISTRATION FEE: A minor charge by the company for completing the transfer of securities. It is not always levied.

RENUNCIATION: A new issue of securities, either by application in a new issue or by rights to an existing shareholder, will be effected first by an allotment letter, with a renunciation form attached. During the renunciation period the rights to these shares may be sold.

RESERVES: In the books of a company, reserves represent the balance of the net assets for shareholders in addition to the nominal value of the share capital. The distinction between share capital and reserves is purely one of account. A scrip issue, or 'capitalisation of reserves', will alter the relationship but not the total. The total is itself a reflection of all the real assets in the rest of the balance sheet, minus the liabilities.

RETENTIONS (or retained profits): The amount of the company's annual profit, after all deductions including the dividend to shareholders. In the absence of any special items, retentions are the only item out of annual trading which add to the company's net assets.

RIGHTS ISSUE: An issue of new shares to existing shareholders in a fixed proportion to their holdings, usually at a price which is below the current market price of existing shares. See Vendor Placing.

RISK: A word of various interpretations. Broadly, the amount which one stands to lose in any investment or group of investments. It is closely correlated with the amount one stands to gain, i.e., the reward. Modern investment theorists have attempted to measure the risks of individual shares or groups of shares by tracking their historical performance. Those whose fluctuations are greater than average are said to have high risk. This 'risk' has even been analysed into component parts: 'specific risk', which is to do with the individual characteristics of the company; and 'systematic risk', which is how much the share is geared to general market movements (i.e. does it go up more than average when the market rises, and vice versa). There is no doubt that 'growth shares', on low yields, offer higher risk in this sense. They can rise more in a bull market but drop further in a bear market. In the long term, if they stay growing, the reward will be greater; but buying at the wrong time can be unprofitable.

●

SCRIP ISSUE: A free issue to existing shareholders in some set proportion to the holding. In reality, merely an adjustment to the number of shares, not to their total value.

SEPON: This stands for Stock Exchange Pool Nominees. It is the official nominee company which holds all stock sold during the course of settlement. It makes the task of sorting out the ultimate allocation of stock much easier.

SETTLEMENT: The process of settling the accounts on the final position, after the Stock Exchange Account is over, between all members of the Stock Exchange and their clients.

SETTLEMENT DAY: Also known as Account Day. This is the day by which all accounts have to be paid.

SHOP: The house responsible for the most influential dealings in any stock. It may be the merchant bank which supervised the issue of the company's shares, or the appointed stockbroker to the company.

SHORT: 'Selling short' is selling a security which one does not hold in the hope of buying it back at a lower price. (See Bear.)

SHORTS: Short-dated Government stock, i.e. with a life of less than five years.

SOURCES AND APPLICATION OF FUNDS: This is a table which is now standard in most company annual reports, usually found after the profit and loss account and the balance sheets. It lists, first, all the main sources of funds over the year. This includes not only the trading profit, as in the profit and loss account, but also things like proceeds of asset sales and new issues of capital. Then it lists the application of these funds. Again, this will include profit and loss items such as taxation and dividends; but in addition it will list the purchases of capital equipment, the purchase of stock and other expenditures. Finally, we see the balance, which is what has happened to the group's liquidity (i.e. whether its cash has risen or fallen, its overdraft reduced or increased). This table is a useful addition to the accounts, especially in a company with problems over its borrowings.

STAG: Someone who subscribes to a new issue, not to keep the shares, but to make a quick profit when dealings in the shares begin.

STAMP DUTY: Transfer Stamp Duty, imposed by the Government, is payable by the buyer only. It is an *ad valorem* duty, currently 0.5 per cent on UK shares. It is not levied on gilt-edged stocks, company debentures and loan stocks, and certain other securities.

STOCK: One specific meaning is the denomination of a security in units of £100, as with gilts and loan stocks. It is also widely used as an alternative word for share.

STOCKS: The goods and materials held by a company for the purpose of trading. The Americans use the term inventories, and this is becoming more common in the UK.

●

TALISMAN: Stock Exchange's computerised transfer system covering most UK shares.

TAP: Stock Exchange jargon for a stock where there is a continuous supply of sellers, thus keeping the price lower that it would otherwise be. There are certain gilt-edged stocks where the Government, through its own agencies, maintains a tap to control day-to-day price movements.

TECHNICAL ANALYSIS: The name applied to the study of share behaviour with the aim of anticipating future movements. Charts play a large part in this but other aspects of share activity also feature.

TENDER: A method of issuing securities whereby a minimum price is set but investors may bid at prices above this. The subsequent allocation of stock is made at the best price given the volume of application at various levels. It is a form of issue which can create difficulties if not judged correctly.

TRADED OPTION: An option (see entry) which itself is quoted in the Traded Options Market in similar manner to a share.

TRADING PROFIT: The company profit before financial items are deducted, such as interest, directors' and auditors' fees. Nowadays, it is usual to regard trading profit as virtually just the profit before interest.

TRANSFER DEED: The document which the seller of a registered stock must sign to legalise the deal. Non-registered stock (such as bearer securities) does not need a transfer deed.

TRUST: A body set up, under the law governing trusts, to look after the property or investment of other persons. This does not necessarily entail the management of the assets, but responsibility for such management.

TRUSTEE INVESTMENTS: If not otherwise specified, trustees must follow investment policies laid down by the Trustee Investments Act, 1961. The Act obliges trustees to maintain part of their investments in Government stocks and similar securities; it also lays down criteria as to what shares are not eligible for purchase. Shares must be quoted on a recognised Stock Exchange in the UK, the company must have an issued capital of more than £1m, and it must have paid a dividend on all the shares for five years in succession. The rules do not come to grips with the real risks of investment and the running of balanced portfolios.

●

UNDERWRITING: A new issue is normally 'underwritten', for a commission, by the issuing house responsible for it to the company involved. It is a guarantee that the shares will be 'taken up', even if the issue is not fully subscribed by the existing shareholders or the public. In turn, the underwriter will engage 'sub-underwriters', usually a spread of institutions to share the risk for a share in the commission.

UNFRANKED INCOME: See Franked Income.

UNIT TRUST: A trust formed to manage securities for the holders of the units. The trust deed defines the terms of operation. The trustee, often one of the big banks, is the legal holder of the securities involved and acts as their custodian. The managers look after the practical investment details. Most of the big unit trust management groups perform all the administrative and investment functions. The Department of Trade exercises control over unit trusts in various ways, including how units may be sold to the public. In return, 'authorised' unit trusts (most UK-based trusts in fact) gain certain tax advantages, including freedom from capital gains tax on their portfolio transactions.

UNLISTED SECURITIES MARKET: This was an innovation of the Stock Exchange in 1980. It is a market for shares in companies which cannot fulfil all the requirements of the Stock Exchange for a full quotation. They do have to comply with regulations on disclosure of information once they are quoted on the USM.

UNQUOTED SECURITIES: Shares which are dealt in by the market but which are not subject to any requirements at all and give no official status. Certain rules have been established to cover these unofficial dealings. Rule 163(2) was designed to cover occasional transactions in small companies. Rule 163(3) was designed to cover new ventures in such fields as oil exploration.

●

VENDOR PLACING: A placing of shares held by some person or persons who have acquired them as payment for the purchase of their company. A form of financing which substitutes for a rights issue, but gives no 'pre-emptive' rights of subscription to existing shareholders.

●

WITHHOLDING TAX: Tax deducted from dividends paid by foreign companies to non-residents. 15 per cent is a common figure. Individual investors can reclaim this tax in the case of most major countries.

WORKING CAPITAL: Often used instead of the term 'net current assets', i.e. current assets minus current liabilities.

●

YIELD: The return offered on the current market price of a security by the annual gross interest or the latest gross annual dividend. Thus, it is the interest or dividend, divided by the market price, as a percentage. (See also Current Yield, Redemption Yield and Earnings Yield).

'YIELD GAP': Traditionally the difference between the yield on 2½ per cent Consols, an old established undated gilt-edged stock, and the average yield on shares. More recently, the average yield on long-dated gilts has been used instead of that on Consols. Before 1960, gilt yields were less than the average equity yield. But since then the position has been reversed, gilts yielding more than equities.

Index